# Super Charge Your Brain

## By Dr. David Jockers

**Co Authors:**
Kevin Krautsack & Steve Sisk (Research Assistants)
Kelcie Yeo (Recipes)

SuperCharge Your Brain

Copyright©2013 by Dr. David Jockers
All rights reserved
International Standard Book Number:

No part of this publication may be copied or reproduced without prior permission from the author.

ISBN-10:0985081074
ISBN-13:9780985081072

Printed in USA by The Warehouse

# Table of Contents

Endorsements……………………………………………………4

Acknowledgments………………………………………………6

Dedication ……………………………………………………….7

SuperCharge Your Brain……………………………………… 8

SuperCharge Your Life……………………………………….11

Brain Boosting Nutrients…………………………………….. 14

Brain Destroying Poisons……………………………………. 17

26 SuperFoods to SuperCharge Your Brain……………….23

Chronic Stress Damages Brain Function………………….33

Brain Based Movement & Exercise   …………………….36

SuperCharged Mindset……………………………………….44

SuperCharged Brain Strategies……………………………..48

Brain Boosting Supplements………………………………..63

 The SuperCharged Lifestyle………………………………..68

SuperBrain Recipes…………………………………………..69

Research……………………………………………..95-111

3

# Endorsements

"Every important electronic in your house has a manual. The most important organ in the body is your brain. It controls everything, and yet this world is lacking a manual on how to optimize the focus, clarity and health of the brain. This practical brain manual will not just help you maximize brain function but will help you lose weight faster and skyrocket your energy. It's never too late to start... or too early. I recommend it to anyone with a brain."

Dr. Isaac H. Jones, *Founder of DesignerHealthCenters.com*

"Dr. David Jockers thirst and ability to effectively communicate the "super charged life" that can be achieved through natural health strategies makes him not only a must read in the nations top health blogs and websites but now as an author of "Super Charge Your Brain" readers will receive the complete formula for brain health, memory, sharpness and capacity that will expand even the most dedicated natural health enthusiasts tool kit for a Super Charged Life."

Warren Phillips - CEO of Health Centers of the Future

"If you want to increase your energy, burn fat, and improve your brain function then Super Charge Your Brain is the book for you. Dr. Jockers covers a range of topics from super foods to brain boosting foods that have been proven through science and patient success stories. Dr. Jockers is an incredible writer and gives you an in-depth nutritional wisdom but yet keeps it simple enough that anyone can understand the advice and apply it to their life. If you want a book that is revolutionary and yet backed by ancient wisdom, then you are going to love Super Charge Your Brain!"

Dr. Josh Axe -Author Real Food Diet Cookbook
Author – The Dr Axe Detox

"If you want to take your brain, your health and your life to the next level than I would highly suggest practicing the principles found in Dr. David Jockers' new book "Super Charge Your Brain."

> Jordan Rubin NMD, PhD
> New York Times Bestselling Author The Maker's Diet
> Founder Garden of Life and Beyond Organic

"Dr. David Jockers serves as a perfect example of where modern medicine is heading. I know you will benefit greatly from the information contained in his latest book – "Super Charge Your Brain." Be sure to share this information with your family and friends – it could just save their life."

> Jonathan Landsman, NaturalHealth365.com

"I've never met anyone, young, old, or in-between who cares as much about people as Dr. J does. He knows how important our health is to us, and to God, and never stops trying to challenge us to be wise and take ownership of it."

> Suzanne Roberts, Author of "It's Time to Power Up!"

Dr. Jockers not only bases his book on scientific evidence and patient testimonials, but cutting edge efforts that have been shocking clinicians around the world. Having worked with him on countless seminars and witnessed his efforts in research, I can say without question that his pursuit of truth in wellness is unparalleled. Supercharge Your Brain is not a book simply about brain function, but about all things under your brain… Everything! -

Dr. Eric Richards, HealthSprout, President of The Garage Games

**Dedication:**

This book is dedicated to all those who are passionate about living their full God-given potential in life and health.

Dr. David Jockers

# Acknowledgments

I would like to thank my co-authors Kevin Krautsack and Steve Sisk for their great efforts in accumulating the research behind this book. These two are some of the youngest and brightest minds in the natural health movement. Your future clients are blessed to have you guys as their doctor and health coaches. Praying for an amazing future helping many people get well naturally and achieving their health potential.

Thank you to Kelcie Yeo and Megan Kelly for your AMAZING recipes combining the greatest superfoods into creative and tasty dishes. You are both extremely talented, creative, fun and a blessing to work with.

Thank you to Jo Ann Josey for your dedication and support to helping me get this book published. I am forever grateful for your efforts and commitment to excellence with this project.

Thank you to my mom and dad and the rest of my family for your constant encouragement and support. Love you guys!

Thank you to my AWESOME team at Exodus Health Center. Dr Shannon Good, Dr Andrew St Bernard, Diane Walker, Renee Claire Gautron and Terri Connor. You guys have blessed me with the freedom to be able to have a world-class health clinic that saves lives locally every day while pursuing my passion of reaching a broader audience with my writing. Thank you!

Much love to all of my health clients past, present and future who have trusted me and followed my recommendations. It is through you that I have had the opportunity to learn much in regards to leadership, healing, faith and life. It is still my greatest joy to see people achieve new breakthroughs in their life and health. I have been so blessed by so many of you who have had the discipline and focus to change your lives and achieve extraordinary health.

# Chapter One

# SuperCharge Your Brain

Have you ever had trouble staying focused, paying attention and getting things done? I know I have. Teachers and medical professionals would have easily classified me with an attention deficit disorder as I always had challenges sitting still and focusing.

I also struggled with fatigue. Growing up I was always tired. It didn't matter how much sleep I got or how much rest and relaxation I experienced. Once I got back into the grind…the fatigue and tiredness always came back. My mind was all over the place and it was hard to concentrate on any one thing at a time.

As I started college this became an even greater challenge trying to study and remember the information I needed to perform well on tests. Finally, it all culminated with me getting sick with severe digestive cramping and irritable bowel syndrome.

## My Road Back

As I studied the health issues I was struggling with, I realized that my diet and lifestyle were causing the problems. I began incorporating the brain boosting strategies I discuss in this book and my entire life transformed.

Not only was I able to study and retain the information I was learning in school but I had incredible energy that allowed me to work two jobs throughout my time in school. I ended up receiving awards for academic excellence in my undergraduate program and was salutatorian of my graduate class at Life University in Marietta, Georgia.

I then went on to open Exodus Health Center in Kennesaw, Georgia where I have had tremendous success helping people transform their lifestyles and improve their health. I have had the amazing privilege of writing for some of the most notable natural health newsletters and have a syndicated radio show "SuperCharge Your Health" in the Atlanta area.

I even had the opportunity to go to the 2012 Olympic Games and be a part of the performance enhancement team with Maximized Living that helped several athletes improve their lifestyles and athletic prowess on their way to winning Olympic medals.

**From Left to Right:** Dr Jockers with Kayla Harrison Gold Medal winning Judo Athlete    Bronze medal Judo athlete Marti Malloy and Gold Medal winning wrestler Jordan Burroughs.

## The Brain Fog Epidemic

Low energy, poor memory and brain fog are major problems for many individuals. Lowered cognitive function results in lowered working efficiency, relationship disputes and significantly reduced quality of life. Millions of children and adults in America today struggle with mental fatigue, learning, reading & attention challenges. Much of this could be remedied if these individuals knew how to take care of their body and maximize their brain energy.

## Boost Your Families IQ with Natural Lifestyle Strategies

The United States has an epidemic of childhood neurodevelopmental disease such as autism, ADHD, Asperger's and mental retardation. Much of this is due to the influence of industrial chemicals, processed foods, birth and childhood spinal trauma, & sedentary behavior. A lifestyle built around holistic principles can dramatically benefit brain development and improve learning processes.

As a physician, I have had the privilege of working with thousands of individuals with numerous different health conditions. I have worked with elite Olympic level athletes, stay at home moms, busy executives, grandparents and students. I have found that mental fatigue and poor concentration are some of the greatest hindrances for these individuals as they pursue their goals and dreams.

This book is designed to help you unlock your full potential by *SuperCharging Your Brain*.

## Chapter Two

# SuperCharge Your Life

Like a battery...you need to be charged up every day. At the atomic level, our bodies run through an electrical energy system. The coordinated flow of this electrical energy at all times is what makes up the presence of life. Lifestyle habits that add voltage to our system help sustain the flow of energy while habits that subtract voltage reduce the presence of life.

Your body is made up of 75 trillion cells that operate in synchrony to keep you breathing, healing and living every single day. Each of these cells acts as a little battery cranking out energy in the form of a biological unit called adenosine triphosphate (ATP)

The solar power of the sun charges most all life on earth and directly and indirectly charges our bodies. The grassy fields, the trees, the seawater algae and the herbs are living agents that harvest the sun's light through the process of photosynthesis. When we or any other animal consumes these foods we take in the sun's energy as electrons. These electrons are then used to produce energy.

As we increase the amount of electrons through our diet and lifestyle, we build an energy surplus and a stronger life force. This electron flow improves the process of healing, remodeling and rejuvenation within the body.

Unfortunately, in our society today most individuals are deficient in electrons and produce dirty energy. Dirty production creates energy but also a high level of waste in the form of free radical particles. Excessive free radical formation is the anti-thesis to healing and rejuvenation.

When these free radicals are able to run rampant in our bodies they restrict our life force and accelerate aging and tissue degeneration. Anti-oxidants act to neutralize these dangerous free radicals and bring balance to the body.

Certain lifestyle habits produce anti-oxidant rich clean energy while others produce free-radical loaded dirty energy.

## Understanding the Brain & Creative Thinking

In biological sciences, the 1990's were considered the ***"decade of the brain."*** So much research has been done to better understand the brain and nervous system. One key understanding is that the brain acts much like a muscle in its growth and development patterns. This means that the brain depends on fuel and activation in order to adapt and become more proficient in its function.

Creative thinking is one of the greatest human assets in that it initiates new thoughts and world changing ideas. Creativity is the ability to generate ideas of both novel and useful form to a particular social setting. Innovative thoughts inspire excitement and unlock the depths of human potential.

Life is dull, bland and stale without the ability to be creative. The unrestricted human mind has the ability to solve problems with new ideas that build off of the latest technology of the day. In fact, nearly every problem mankind has ever faced has been solved by a new, more creative way of thinking and living.

## Real World Implications for Creative Thinking

Professional athletes have big incentives to perform at an elite level every time they participate in their sport. Business people, doctors, scientists and others have incentive to perform at their highest level every time they step foot into their specific arena. The ability to think quickly and innovatively is one of the characteristics that allow these individuals to have extraordinary success in their field. This ability also offers individuals the opportunity to adapt and evolve to a higher level in every aspect of life.

Therapies and ergonomic aids such as caffeine, herbs, and medications have been used for many years to help individuals perform better in their particular field. Many of these aids provide short term benefits but hinder the health of the individual in the long-term. There are natural performance aids that benefit the individual with very low risk of danger or unwanted side-effects. These brain boosting nutrients are valuable commodities.

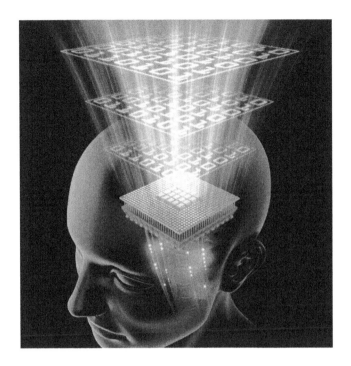

## Chapter Three

# Brain Boosting Nutrients

Your Brain Depends on several key nutrients in order to function at a high level:

1. **SuperCharged Nutrition Principles** as explained in this book

1. **Effective Hydration:** *Brain is 80% water* - drink at least half your body weight in clean water daily.

2. **High Level Oxygen Consumption and Utilization** through a regular exercise program.

3. **Novel Movement Stimulation:** Holistic movements incorporating balance and stability.

4. **Joint & Spinal Proprioception:** Full Range of motion in all joints is an essential brain nutrient that feeds the cerebellum, hippocampus and frontal cortex.

5. **Sunlight:** Vitamin D3 has been shown to be a powerful immune and endocrine modulator. Regular sunlight and vitamin D3 supplementation is very important for optimal health

6. **Rest:** 7-9 hours daily.

7. **Effective Cellular Detoxification:** Optimal glutathione levels

8. **Gratitude, Love and Laughter**

9. **Purpose Driven Thinking**

Your brain absolutely needs all 10 of these vital components. If any of these is compromised the resulting brain function will suffer.

## Brain Boosting Nutrition Principles

Our brain depends upon some critical nutrients that must come from our diet. While most natural, non-processed foods have the potential to improve our cognitive abilities, certain foods are extraordinarily powerful in their ability to boost brain function!

The brain tissue is primarily comprised of water and fatty acids. Therefore, the two most important dietary components to a healthy brain are: Clean Water and Clean Fats. Be sure to build your diet around healthy fat sources as explained in this book and drink at least half your body weight in ounces of clean water.

Beyond that, the brain tissue is extremely vulnerable to free-radical and inflammatory attack. In order to protect the brain from oxidative stress, a diet rich in high-quality anti-oxidants is crucial.

**Antioxidant Rich Foods**: This would include dark green veggies such as collard greens, kale, Swiss chard, spinach, broccoli, and many others. These nutrient dense foods donate an unpaired electron to cancel out the dangerous free radicals and free roaming metabolites. A diet rich in anti-oxidants has been shown to improve brain function substantially. Here are some of the best:

**Berries:** Blueberries, Raspberries, Strawberries are rich in vitamin C & other major phytochemicals that act as powerful anti-oxidants while also being low-glycemic and anti-inflammatory in nature. Be sure to get these organic as they have a thin skin and will be loaded with chemicals if they are conventional.

**Vitamin E:** Organic eggs, Extra-virgin olive oil, Almonds, Brazil nuts, Sunflower seeds, Pumpkin Seeds & Hemp Seeds.

**Glutathione Rich Foods:** Glutathione is the body's master intracellular (within the cell) anti-oxidant that helps protect the DNA

and flush toxins out of the cell. Low glutathione levels would indicate poor cellular detoxification and DNA damage. The best whole food sources include:
1) Non-Denatured, grass-fed whey protein

1) Raw, grass-fed cheese and Organic Eggs

2) Avocados, Spinach and Asparagus

**Best Brain Based Fats:** The matter of the brain is 70% fat, therefore, outside of water this makes fat the most critical nutrient in the brain. Here are the necessary fats that help to make a healthy brain:

**Saturated Fats:** Extra-Virgin Coconut Oil, Grass-fed meats.

**Alkaline Forming Fats:** Extra-Virgin Olive Oil, Avocados, Almonds, Pecans and Pumpkin Seeds.

**Omega 3 Fats:** High quality Fish Oil, Krill Oil, Grass-Fed Meats, Wild Fish, Flax Oil, Flax seeds, Hemp seeds, Chia seeds, Pumpkin seeds and Walnuts.

**GLA:** Gamma-Linoleic Acid in Borage Oil, Evening Primrose Oil, Black Currant and Hemp Oil and Seeds.

This book will explain more details about how to get these nutrients into your diet on a regular basis.

# Chapter Four

# Brain Destroying Poisons

The brain is extremely sensitive to free radical damage, poor circulation and poor blood sugar balance. Individuals with chronic inflammatory stress, arterial restriction and blood sugar imbalances will have trouble with memory and brain fog.

These are some of the most potent toxins for the brain and neurological tissue.

1. **Gluten**: One of the most common nutritional/toxicity issues in our society today deals with the common protein found in wheat, barley, rye, oats, kamut and spelt. According to gluten researcher Kenneth Fine, up to 81% of our society has a gluten allergy. When exposed to gluten the body has differing degrees of inflammatory responses. Some individuals have mild inflammatory reactions while others have severe reactions.

   The most vulnerable tissue to the inflammatory cascade in response to gluten is the brain and nervous system. The immune molecules that are secreted (cytokines) destroy brain tissue and cause massive neurological damage. The most common symptoms associated with this reaction are brain fog, memory problems and mental fatigue.

1. **Unfermented Soy**: One of soy's primary isoflavones, genistein, has been shown to inhibit the enzyme tyrosine kinase in the brain. The highest amounts of tyrosine kinases are found in the hippocampus, a brain region that is essential to learning and memory. High soy consumption actually blocks this mechanism of memory formation.

   Several studies have associated high intakes of tofu and other unfermented soy products to increased risk of dementia and cognitive impairments. On the flip side, fermented soy products such as tempeh and miso are associated with greater cognitive abilities. Researchers hypothesize that this is due to the deep fermentation process removing enzyme inhibitors and phytoestrogens. In addition, this process increases folate, which is a critical nutrient for brain and nervous system function.

2. **Blood Sugar Imbalance**: The brain depends on a continual supply of glucose for energy. A 2003 study in the Proceedings of the National Academy of Sciences found that people's memory is harmed by poor blood sugar metabolism. Stable blood sugar levels are critical for healthy brain and neuronal cells that fire quickly and efficiently. Abnormal blood sugar levels also cause neuronal damage and weaken the protective blood-brain barrier. This makes for easy passage of different toxins and other particles that will disrupt brain function.

A mechanism for Alzheimer's disease is that of poor blood sugar metabolism. This pre-diabetic disorder opens the door in the blood brain barrier for toxic aluminum particles to cross-over and accumulate in the sensitive regions of the temporal lobe.

## Fructose Sugar is Toxic for the Brain

Fructose is a form of sugar that has also been shown to be highly toxic to brain tissue. Fructose is the most common sugar found in fruit as well as processed foods. The brain runs off of glucose but has trouble processing fructose. Fructose causes cellular inflammation that damages insulin receptors and distorts blood sugar signaling.

A study conducted at UCLA showed that rats fed a diet high in fructose performed significantly worse than control groups and glucose fed rats in their ability to navigate a maze. Other research has shown that fructose distorts the brain's energy metabolism in areas of the hippocampus that are related with memory consolidation. Thus the assumption has been made that high fructose consumption is related to memory loss and dementia.

3. **Fluoride**: Elevated fluoride consumption has been shown to reduce IQ in children. Cognitive ability is further reduced if the individual is deficient in iodine. Fluoride consumption as low as 1part per million (ppm) has been shown to impair neurological anti-oxidant defense systems and damage areas of the hippocampus, pineal gland & cerebellum. Typical tap water contains close to 1ppm of fluoride. Fluoride is also associated with increased uptake of aluminum into brain tissue. Fluoride intake has been shown to increase the formation of amyloid plaques in the brain. Both the elevated aluminum and amyloid plaques are characteristically found in Alzheimer's disease.

The most common sources of fluoride are through municipal water sources, fluoride based toothpaste, & processed foods and drinks. Certain medications and commercial cleaning products may also contain fluoride.

4. **Toxic Fats**: High Omega 6 fats & hydrogenated vegetable oils (trans-fats). French researchers in 1994 found that dietary trans fatty acids did indeed find their way into the myelin (outer layer) of brain cells, where they changed the electrical conductivity of the cells.

Furthermore, this study published in the journal "Lipids" demonstrated that trans-fats compete with Omega 3 fats for location spots in the cell membrane. Several studies have indicated that trans-fatty acid uptake into the cell membranes is twice as high when omega 3 fatty acids are deficient as compared to when there is adequate amounts of omega 3 fatty acids.

Even worse for the brain is when we are eating trans-fats during pregnancy. A 1996 Canadian study showed that the average lactating woman had 7.2% of the fatty acids in their breast milk being trans-fatty acids. These trans-fats have a powerful affinity for the neuronal cell membrane.

This study published in "Lipids," demonstrated that trans-fats consumed location spots on the neuronal cell membrane, inhibiting omega 3 fatty acids EPA & DHA from their vital membrane functions. This process caused a structural and functional change in the cell leading to chemical and electrical imbalances in the brain.

5. **Sedentary Living & Poor Posture:** The brain depends on oxygen and activation from muscle and joint receptors on a continual basis. A lack of motion results in a significant reduction in oxygen uptake and delivery into the spinal cord and brain.

Poor posture and subluxated spinal vertebrae cause spinal joint receptors to fire abnormal, corrupted patterns into the brain. This causes further brain-body feedback problems and disrupted movement patterns in the body. Chronically poor posture is one of the most detrimental factors for brain function.

6. **Tap Water:** Municipal water is extraordinarily toxic to healthy brain development. This water is loaded with environmental toxins such as chlorine, DBP's, heavy metals and fluoride. Proper water filtration is essential to remove these chemical agents.

High quality reverse osmosis systems are one of the very few water systems that is able to effectively remove fluoride. Add back a pinch of pink salt (1/4 teaspoon per gallon) to replace any lost minerals from the reverse osmosis process. Teach your children not to use municipal water fountains but instead to carry bottled water in either glass or stainless steel bottles.

7. **Heavy Metals**: The major heavy metals that are found in human brain tissue include mercury and aluminum. Both of

these are extremely toxic and cause major free radical stress and inflammation that chews up neurological tissue.

The major exposure areas for these heavy metals include the following:

| | |
|---|---|
| Dental Amalgam Fillings | Vaccines |
| Seafood | Processed Foods |
| Tap Water | Processed Juices & Drinks |
| Certain Medications | Industrial Waste |

8. **Poor Sleeping Habits**: Quality sleep is one of the most fundamental nutrients that every person needs in order to perform at their optimal. Sleep deprivation creates a heightened stress response within the body that disrupts normal healing and tissue rejuvenation processes.

Sleep deprivation dramatically reduces human growth hormone secretion and testosterone production. Both of these hormones are responsible for tissue healing and boosting metabolism to burn fat and build muscle as well as for providing a healthy immune response.

Sleep deprivation causes a decrease in lean body tissue, an increase in fat storage and decreased immune coordination. Lowered immune coordination increases inflammatory processes and increases the susceptibility to auto-immune conditions.

Memory performance has been shown to be significantly reduced in sleep deprived individuals. Coordination, balance and reaction time are also known to be reduced in chronically sleep deprived individuals.

Be sure to get as close to eight hours of sleep each night to ensure proper healing and cognitive function. Researchers believe that every hour of sleep before midnight has the equivalent tissue healing properties as three hours of sleep after midnight. So look to get to bed early. Great hours of sleep are 9pm-5am, 10pm-6am or 11pm to 7am.

9. **Toxic Emotions**: Destructive thinking creates free radical damage in the brain and rewires a chronic stress response in the body. Toxic emotions include fear, anger, bitterness, unforgiveness, depression; low self-worth, etc. hardwire the brain for low energy and create massive inflammatory damage to the neurological system.

The average person has over 30,000 thoughts a day! Research shows that destructive thoughts trigger more than 1,400 known physical and chemical responses and activates more than 30 different hormones. Toxic waste generated by destructive thoughts degenerates the brain.

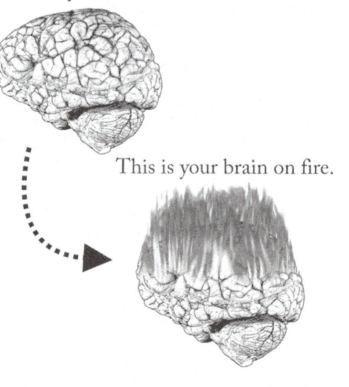

This is your brain.

This is your brain on fire.

## Chapter Five

# 26 SuperFoods to SuperCharge Your Brain

There are many great superfoods that enhance brain function and I could have written a whole manual just on these unique foods. Instead, I decided to take 26 that I utilize regularly that have had a great effect on my own life. Here they are:

**Apple Cider Vinegar (ACV):** ACV is a powerful tonic loaded with incredible living nutrients. The ACV should be raw, unpasteurized with the "mother" intact. The mother is the portion of the apple that is fermented and contains the source of the good bacteria and enzymes. These enzymes help the body heal and digest nutrients from other foods.

ACV is also a rich source of organic acids which help with insulin sensitivity and decreasing inflammation. The good bacteria enhance nutrient assimilation and overall gut function. Use ACV on meat, brown rice, vegetables and other foods. It can also be put into a variety of different drinks for added anti-oxidants and enzymes.

**Ashwagandha:** This exotic herb has powerful antioxidant properties that protect the brain and nervous system. Premature aging associated with chronic tension on the nervous system is related to increased oxidative stress. In the largest human trial using ashwagandha the herb was shown to reduce cortisol levels up to 26%. Chronically elevated cortisol increases inflammatory and degenerative processes in the body.

This herb has been shown in studies to have as strong an anti-anxiety and anti-depressant effect as leading name brand medications. Ashwagandha has been shown to support the regeneration and reconstruction of nerve cells and synapses. This suggests that ashwagandha could help reverse states of brain and nervous system degeneration. This makes it a potent defense against dementia, Alzheimer's disease and other neurodegenerative disorders.

You can get Ashwagandha as a fresh or dried herb or in organic herbal teas. You can also use it in whole food based supplements.

**Avocados:** This amazing fruit is very high in healthy oleic acid. This is a monounsaturated fat that helps increase fat metabolism. It is also rich in the powerful carotenoid anti-oxidants lutein and zeaxanthin as well as
vitamin E (tocopherol).

These anti-oxidants decrease oxidative stress and allow for a healthier cellular environment. Other critical components include ionic potassium and folate. These elements are alkaline forming in the body and help to buffer acidic wastes that accumulate within the bloodstream.

**Blueberries:** This summer superfood is loaded with antioxidant phytonutrients called anthocyanidins. These nutrients powerfully neutralize free radical damage to the collagen matrix of cells and tissues. In addition, anthocyanidins have been shown to improve capillary integrity and enhance the effects of Vitamin C.

The anti-oxidant power of blueberries has been shown to be particularly useful in stabilizing brain function and protecting the neural tissue from oxidative stress. Studies have shown improvements in memory and learning while reducing symptoms of depression.

**Cacao**: This favorite superfood is rich in epicatechin which is a powerful polyphenol anti-oxidant. It also contains theobromine which is a natural cardiovascular stimulant that enhances blood flow to the brain. Theobromine is both safe and non-addictive and has shown clinical benefits with improved memory and cognitive processing

**Chia Seeds:** Chia is made up of healthy fats, anti-oxidants clean proteins and fiber. Chia contains no sugar and very minimal amounts of non-fibrous carbohydrates. Chia also contains high levels of calcium, magnesium and potassium. This combination is perfect for healthy blood sugar levels and sustained energy.

Chia is loaded with omega 3 fatty acids and nueroprotective anti-oxidants such as quercetin, caffeic and chlorogenic acid. These essential fats and anti-oxidants produce cell membranes that are more flexible and efficient. Healthier cell membranes results in more efficient nutrient delivery systems and faster nerve transmission processes. This improves brain function including memory and concentration.

**Cinnamon**: This is one of the most anti-oxidant rich herbs that also has a major effect on improving blood sugar stability. The anti-oxidants within cinnamon help protect the neurons from free radical stress and stimulate insulin receptors which allows for greater blood sugar stabilization. Improved blood sugar stability results in improved brain energy, memory and creativity.

**Citrus Bioflavonoids**: These unique phytonutrients which are together classified as vitamin P have shown to improve capillary permeability and blood flow. This helps to oxygenate the deep regions of the brain that are critical for cognitive processing and sensory acuity. Fresh squeezed lemon and citrus essential oils are rich in these bioflavonoids.

**Eggs:** This is one of the best foods for healthy brain function. Eggs are a major source of the brain enhancing B vitamin choline. According to Iowa State researchers in 2007, 90% of the American population is choline deficient. Egg yolks and egg based lecithin's are some of the richest and most bioavailable sources of choline.

Choline is important for the brain for several reasons. It helps to produce phosphatidylcholine and sphingomyelin. These two molecules make up a particularly high percentage of the brain's total mass. Choline also helps to form a critical neurotransmitter in the brain called acetylcholine. Acetylcholine is the body's primary molecule for sending messages between nerves & muscles.

Choline also helps protect the body's stores of folate which is a key B vitamin for the development and maintenance of the nervous system. Finally, choline has important anti-inflammatory properties called methylation. This process of methylation plays a significant role in many chemical events which actually turn certain genes on and off in the body.

**Fermented Raw Dairy**: Raw cheese and fermented whole milk from 100% grass-fed cows is loaded with brain boosting omega 3 fatty acids. It also contains tons of Conjugated Linoleic Acid (CLA), which is a great brain protectant fatty acid.

Some of the best products include raw, 100% grass-fed cow and goat cheeses, Amasi, fermented whey and kefir. These dairy products contain highly bioavailable calcium and magnesium, amino acids and vitamin A, D3 and K2. It also is an outstanding source of sulfur groups that enhance the brain's ability to detoxify effectively. Be sure your dairy is from 100% grass-fed cows! It must say this on the label or it is from grain-fed cows and is not healthy.

**Ginger**: This is an important part of a de-inflaming, natural pain-relief program. The compound 6-gingerol has been shown to significantly inhibit the production of a highly reactive nitrogen molecule, nitric oxide, which quickly forms a dangerous free radical peroxynitrite. Additionally, ginger helps to protect the body's stores of glutathione – the master anti-oxidant.

Ginger is also very high in potassium which aids in electrical energy production and detoxification. It is a great source of manganese which protects the lining of key blood vessels that oxygenate and bring fuel to the brain. Manganese deficiencies can lead to dementia and stroke.

**Gingko Biloba**: Nicknamed the "memory herb" it works by dilating blood vessels going to the brain to increase blood flow into the region. This increases oxygen, removes hazardous waste products and neutralizes dangerous free radicals.

Several different studies have showed that ginkgo can improve memory and attention span in healthy individuals with peak performance coming about 2 hours after ingestion. Ginkgo also improves vision and overall eye health as it prevents against macular degeneration, glaucoma and cataracts.

**Green Coffee Bean Extract**: This superfood is loaded with powerful brain enhancing and blood sugar balancing anti-oxidants. These polyphenol anti-oxidants are chlorogenic and caffeic acids which have a powerful effect on enhancing insulin signaling and blood sugar metabolism. Stable blood sugar allows for better energy, mental clarity, hormone function, detoxification capabilities and weight loss.

**Grass-Fed Beef**: This contains omega-3 fatty acids, CLA, saturated fat, vitamin B12 and the powerful anti-oxidant carnosine. These essential fatty acids play an enormous role in the foundation of the neuronal cells that makeup the central nervous system. The brain concentrates carnosine to protect itself from advanced glycolytic enzymes (AGE's) which are the most hazardous free radicals and are linked with neurodegenerative disorders such as Alzheimer's and Parkinson's disease.

**Hemp Seeds:** Hemp seeds is a complete protein and contains an optimal ratio of omega 6:omega 3 fatty acids. Hemp is also a great source of the omega-6 essential fat gamma linoleic acid (GLA). GLA is only found in quantities of significance in hemp, borage oil, evening primrose oil, black currant seed oil & spirulina. Because of the scarcity of GLA much of our society is deficient in this essential fatty acid. GLA is critical for reducing inflammation in our body and is one of the most powerful nutrients for balancing hormones. Additionally, sufficient quantities of GLA promote healthy skin, hair, nails and brain function.

**Holy Basil:** Holy basil is known in natural medicine as an adaptogenic herb in that it helps the body to better adapt to stress. Adaptogenic herbs don't affect an individual's mood but they help the body function at its optimal level during times of stress. They do this by modulating the production of stress hormones like cortisol and adrenaline.

One of the key components that adaptogenic herbs offer is their ability to lower and stabilize cortisol levels. High cortisol drains the precursors to major hormones such as testosterone, progesterone and estrogen. With less than adequate raw materials, the body becomes sex hormone deficient. This process rapidly accelerates the aging process and makes an individual's life miserable.

Healthy individuals have stable cortisol levels that naturally spike in the morning and then level off and stay consistently low during the day before tapering at night. This allows us to wake up with energy in the morning and maintain that energy until nightfall when we should naturally be gearing down and getting ready for sleep. Stable cortisol levels result in improved mental clarity and memory. The individual feels as though they are less agitated and anxious and therefore able to perform better and have higher quality of life.

**Peppermint:** The methanol component of peppermint has also been shown to improve circulation throughout the body. This is especially true in the brain where peppermint oil helps to enhance cognitive processing and stimulate creative thought. Increased circulation in the brain leads to new creative energies and elevated mental stamina and improved memory formation.

**Red Onions:** Are a rich source of the flavonoid anti-oxidant quercetin and the polyphenol anti-oxidant anthocyanin. These anti-oxidants prevent the oxidation of dietary and cellular fatty acids. They are very powerful free radical scavengers that neutralize cancer cell growth and dramatically reduce whole body inflammation.

Red onions are also a fantastic source of chromium which lowers blood sugar and enhances cellular insulin sensitivity. Nearly 50% of the US population is deficient in chromium which is greater than any other developed nation. This is due to over cropping that has stripped the land of chromium and processed food consumption. Chromium deficiencies lead to diabetes, dementia, Alzheimer's and heart disease.

**Rhodiola:** The adaptogenic herb rhodiola enhances serotonin and endorphin activity within the brain. Healthy serotonin levels are necessary to balance our mood and keep us calm and positive. Dopamine drives us towards accomplishing goals and enhances our self-esteem and confidence. Endorphins help us to feel good and lift our mood and spirits.

Rhodiola is known to help people calm their emotions and stimulate cognitive processes that improve memory and creative thinking. Several studies have shown that rhodiola improves associative thinking, speed of audiovisual perception and ability to perform complex calculations. Researchers also found that it significantly reduced stress-induced fatigue after just two weeks of regular usage.

**Rosemary**: This herb is a great brain stimulant that prevents the breakdown of a key neurotransmitter named acetylcholine. This molecule allows the neuronal cells that are responsible for cognitive processing and memory consolidation to communicate more effectively with one another.

**Sea Vegetables:** The term seaweed actually encompasses a number of different "sea weeds" including kelp, nori, dulse, wakame, kombu, arame and many others. Gram for gram, sea vegetables are higher in essential vitamins and minerals than any other known food group. Be sure to get your sea vegetables from a certified organic source to reduce risk of heavy metal exposure.

Sea vegetable contains critical nutrients that benefit brain function and development. This includes folic acid, iodine, choline and omega 3 fatty acids. They also contain unique sulfated polysaccharides called fucoidans that have a powerful anti-inflammatory effect in the body. These minerals are bio-available to the body in chelated, colloidal forms that make them more easily absorbed.

**Spinach:** This food is extremely rich in blood purifying chlorophyll. Chlorophyll is easily metabolized and used to build new red blood cells and pull out carcinogenic substances from the body.

Chlorophyll also provides magnesium which acts to strengthen the blood-brain barrier and protect the neurological system from environmental toxins.

Spinach is an amazing source of glycoclycerolipids that protect the digestive tract from inflammatory damage. These glycoclycerolipids are the main fatty acids that make up the cell membranes of light-sensitive organs in chlorophyll containing plants. Additionally, spinach is an important source of copper, zinc, and selenium which boost brain function.

Spinach also contains some very newly studied carotenoid anti-oxidants called eposyxanthophylls. The unique epoxyxanthophylls that have been researched to show remarkable anti-cancer properties include neoxanthin and violaxanthin. Spinach is also rich in the powerful carotenoid anti-oxidants lutein and zeaxanthin. These phytonutrients are extremely important for healthy vision and brain function.

**Spirulina:** Spirulina contains an incredible array of nutrients that make them a functional whole food for sustaining life without the need for other foods. These algae contain pre-digested protein (in the form of amino acids) for quick absorption and high utilization rates. Spirulina contains essential omega-3 fatty acids such as DHA. Algae, in fact, are the very source that fish, krill and other animals obtain their omega 3's.

Spirulina is a rich source of the tough to find essential omega-6 fat GLA. It also provides nucleic acids (DNA & RNA) that provide a megadose of raw materials for DNA repair. Spirulina is a very rich source of critical B vitamin methylating agents such as B6 and folic acid. Spirulina has an extraordinary array of powerful anti-oxidants in the form of anthocyanins, carotenoids and superoxide dismutase.

**Turmeric:** Turmeric is the 4th highest anti-oxidant rich herb. Turmeric boosts levels of natural intracellular anti-oxidants such as glutathione, superoxide dismutase, and catalase. Boosting intracellular anti-oxidants helps the brain buffer free radical stress and detoxify from environmental stresses.

Turmeric improves blood flow and reduces brain inflammation. The effect of this accelerates cognitive execution and makes you neurologically sharper. The anti-inflammatory effect also protects against neurodegenerative disorders such as Dementia and Parkinson's Disease.

**Wild Alaskan Salmon:** This super seafood is loaded with long-chain omega 3 fatty acids EPA & DHA which are crucial for healthy neurology. Additionally, wild salmon is rich in astaxanthin which not only gives it a characteristic pink color but is also credited with giving the fish its super strength to swim upstream against strong currents.

Astaxanthin is the most powerful anti-oxidant for healthy brain, vision and neurological function. It has the unique ability to cross the blood brain barrier as well as the blood-retinal barrier while most carotenoids do not. This helps protect the brain and eyes from inflammatory damage and reduces the risk for blindness, cataracts, macular degeneration, dementia, Alzheimer's disease and other neurological disorders.

**Non-Denatured Grass-fed Whey Protein:** This protein provides a mega dose of L-glutamine which is a very important amino acid for tissue healing and a strong gastro-intestinal system. Due to inflammatory diets and the overuse of anti-biotics and other medications many children and adults have a very weak gastrointestinal lining. When this lining is damaged, proteins are able to cross into the bloodstream. The body then goes into self-defense against these alien proteins and triggers an inflammatory attack creating food allergies and intolerances.

High quality whey protein also boosts glutathione which is the bodies master anti-oxidant. Glutathione protects cells by neutralizing oxygen molecules before they damage cells. It also boosts natural liver detoxification and protects the arteries, brain, heart and immune cells among others. Children who are deficient in glutathione are much more likely to develop neurodevelopmental disorders such as autism, ADHD and Asperger's.

Quality whey protein also provides highly bioavailable amino acids that help produce lean muscle tissue. This is especially important for active kids and athletes engaging in long practices and physically demanding sports. These amino acids also help produce enzymes that carry out extremely important functions in the body. Active enzymes help metabolize inflammatory wastes and positively influence tissue healing processes.

For More Information on SuperFoods and Brain Boosting SuperFood Recipes go to DrJockers.com

# Chapter Six

# Chronic Stress Damages Brain Function

Many experts have hypothesized that increased stress cycles in the body produce the environment for disease development within the body. Stress can come from a variety of sources in the mental/emotional form, chemical nature and physical realm. When the body is under increased stress it responds by increasing its sympathetic tone. This means the body shunts itself into "fight or flight" survival based mode by altering cardiovascular & hormonal function to get itself ready for dynamic activity.

Increased sympathetic tone causes a release of stress hormones such as adrenalin, epinephrine, and cortisol. This is the same response we get when we are anxious or exercising. This is good if it is for a short period of time; however, when the stress lasts longer than expected it exhausts the body and causes a state of dis-ease to manifest.

## Brain Body Communication Processes

When the brain sends information to the organs, muscles, and tissues of the body, this is called efferent neurological flow. In return, the afferent flow of information includes all the messages sent to the brain from skin, muscle, joint, and organ receptors. This afferent/efferent neurological loop is how the body is able to respond and adapt appropriately to its environment.

Subluxation is a term used to describe mechanical compression and irritation to spinal joints and nerves. Subluxation scrambles the neurological feedback loop by causing altered rhythms of neurological flow. Subluxations are caused by trauma, poor posture, or increased chemical and emotional stresses.

## Subluxation Effects the Brain-Body Connection

Subluxations are a physical stress on the body and therefore increase the sympathetic tone, so the body shunts its energy toward the fight or flight system. If the subluxation(s) are not corrected they continue to produce this increased stress response. This increases stress hormone production and causes greater joint and ligament laxity in the spine and extremities making them more susceptible to injury. Additionally, increased long-term stress on the body greatly accelerates the degenerative processes of the spine and joints leading to osteoarthritis.

The ramifications of increased stress hormones in the body include overworked adrenal glands, lowered immunity, decreased digestive functions, fatigue and blood pressure disturbances. Increased cortisol levels also cause ligament laxity by stripping critical proteins from the tendon and ligament structures. This causes joint weakness throughout the body, including the spine and extremities, making them much more susceptible to injury.

## Chiropractic Resets the Stress Response

Chiropractic adjustments have been shown to normalize spinal afferent/efferent processes to their proper resting tone. This is like hitting the reset button on the computer when it is malfunctioning. The computer is allowed to pause and reprocess itself. Chiropractic adjustments stop the stress response and restores normal hormonal and cardiovascular function to the body. This allows the body to reset itself and begin healing the damage that was done in the body due to chronic stress cycles.

Research has demonstrated that chiropractic adjustments enhance sensorimotor integration. This refers to the body's ability to sense where it is in space and effectively coordinate complex movement patterns. This improves function in both the brain and the body. Improved spatial intelligence translates into better physical and mental balance, coordination and mobility.

Chiropractic adjustments make you think and move with better speed, skill, and finesse. Other studies have shown that chiropractic care improves creative thinking and ignites renewed energy towards everyday tasks and complicated projects. Less physical nerve stress equals greater productivity and life potential. See your chiropractor!

*For More Information on Maximized Living, Chiropractic, Posture & Spinal Exercises go to DrJockers.com for helpful Articles, Podcasts & Videos.

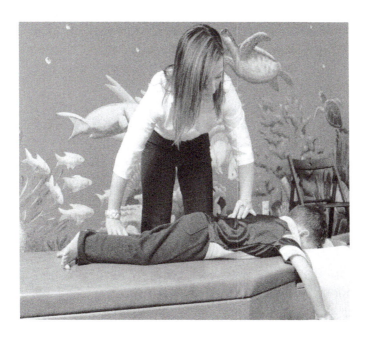

# Chapter Seven

# Brain Based Movement & Exercise

The human brain is the most magnificent of all of creation. The brain consists of an amazing network of high energy microscopic neurons that allow us to think, learn, reason, move and experience our environment. This system is dynamic in that it is constantly growing and adapting.

Areas of the brain are driven through activity. With the right form of movement the brain adapts to become stronger and better able to accomplish daily tasks. Of course, the opposite is true as well. Where there is less activity, there is regression and atrophy. This is the principle of neuroplasticity. The brain is a constantly adapting structure that depends on movement for energy and instruction. "You either use it or you lose it."

## Neuron Communication Processes

Neurons are constantly communicating with each other through electrical impulses and chemical signals. Information travels in the form of electrical impulses and activates messenger chemicals called neurotransmitters. These neurotransmitters flow into the synapse and connect the message to the next series of neurons.

Neurons connect with each other to form networks that carry a tremendous amount of information from one area of the brain to another. Typical neuron networks have over 10,000 synapses. Electrical impulses travel across these neurons at over four hundred miles per hour. This speed allows us to process language, feel inspired, recall a memory and laugh at a joke in a moment's notice.

Brain-based exercises create new and stronger synapses (space between neurons). Synaptic density is associated with greater memory and creativity. The brain synapses begin degenerating after the age of twenty but brain-based exercises help to strengthen these connections.

**Neurobics:** This is a term that was described by the late neurobiologist Lawrence Katz and Manning Rubin. It refers to the physiological effects of unique and non-routine ways of thinking and moving and their effects on the brain. Routine activities become so automatic in the brain that they require less brain activity. Unique activities produce more neurotransmitters and have a greater effect on altering and strengthening neurons and synaptic connections.

Neurobic exercises must be different than typical activities that you do and they can incorporate all of your five senses. Examples of such include:

> Writing or using a utensil with your non-dominant hand
> Walking down your hallway with your eyes closed
> One leg balancing exercises
> Spend time outside smelling all the plants and flowers
> Eat foods with lots of colors to stimulate your visual senses
> Feel the texture of different objects like rocks, shells, etc.

## Other Neurobic Activities:

1) Use essential oils – take a sniff to excite your brain
1) Brush your teeth with non-dominant hand
2) Listening to classical music or music that has different tones, melodies and instruments than you are used to listening too.
3) Surround yourself with lots of different colors
4) Play a new instrument or try a new sporting activity
5) Do a crossword puzzle
6) Walk barefoot outside and pay attention to the unique feel of the rocks and ground with your feet.
7) Sit in a park and journal about all the unique sounds and smells you are experiencing.
8) Read a book or recite a speech out-load while pacing with your eyes closed
   10) Try a new, healthy dish with unique flavors you are not accustomed too.

## The Brain Drives the Muscles

The brain is the most complex and incredible organ on earth. The brain contains 100 billion nerve cells and each of these are interconnected with other nerve cells through hundreds and thousands of other synapses (or little gaps between neurons). There are believed to be more connections within the brain than there are stars in the sky.

The brain drives the skeletal muscles and the skeletal muscles help drive higher brain function. There is such an intimate connection between the brain and muscles that powerful, long-standing emotional memories are known to be released during deep massage and chiropractic care.

Movement deficiency is a leading cause of degenerative disease and early death. Lack of healthy motion causes the neural synapses to atrophy. Sedentary living, poor posture, and bad spinal health accelerate the degenerative processes of the brain.

**Cerebellum: "Little brain,"** constitutes just 10% of the total volume of the brain but amazingly it contains over 50% of the neurons in the entire human brain. The cerebellum's job is to modify and adapt movement patterns to improve coordination and balance. Incredibly, before any movement (even something as simple as bending over to pick up a pen) is even initiated, the cerebellum, through a feed-forward mechanism has already perceived the intended motion up to six times and fires down to contract the core musculature to prepare for the anticipated movement.

**Basal Ganglia:** This is located near the center of the brain and it helps to integrate feelings, thoughts and movement together. This is the part of the brain that has us shake when we are nervous, jump when we are excited and scream when we are scared. The role of the basal ganglia is to give us the correct movement patterns to go with our emotional feelings and perception of our environment. Without proper movement patterns the basal ganglia gets wound up and causes chronic anxiety.

**Limbic System:** This is the emotional brain as it stores our emotional responses to the environment we perceive. It helps to store highly charged emotional responses to the events of our past along with the Temporal lobe. When this part of the brain is tempered or cool we typically flow with positivity. Without proper movement patterns the deep limbic system gets hot and creates a depressive spiral of thinking and behavior. Proper movement is very important to keeping the limbic system balanced and under control.

**Anterior Cingulate Gyrus:** This region of the brain runs lengthwise through the deep aspects of the frontal lobes. This region of the brain allows for cognitive flexibility. This region depends upon the neurotransmitter serotonin. When the body has chronic stress it can lead to a hot anterior cingulate gyrus. This is experienced as worrying and obsessive compulsive behavior. The strategies in this book allow for normalized serotonin levels and a cooling effect of the Anterior Cingulate.

**Hippocampus:** The Memory Center: Movement is essential for a healthy hippocampus and higher levels of memory consolidation. Dynamic exercise that use novel techniques have been shown to rapidly improve memory centers as opposed to standard single-joint exercises. This form of exercise has been shown to increase Growth Factor (IGF) and BDNF (bone-derived neurotropic factor) which are essential for healthy neurons, formation of new neurons, synapses between neurons and increased neuronal learning.

**Frontal Lobe:** The critical center for learning and emotional control. The frontal lobe functions can be remembered with the 3 "T's" for tension, tact, and tenacity. Tension: The unique ability of a human to rise above emotional reactions and selfish/primitive behaviors.

Tact: The ability to understand and apply socially acceptable behaviors. Tenacity: The ability to focus on one thing for a period of time.

Children with ADHD are known to have retarded frontal cortices and thus they have an inability to apply the 3 T's effectively. Brain based exercise, along with nutritional, detoxification and spinal corrective recommendations have been shown to be an extremely powerful tool for individuals with ADHD.

## Full Body – Novel and Challenging Movements

The brain is driven through full body movements that are unique and challenging. Novel exercises that utilize an unstable atmosphere such as balancing on one leg, using a stability ball, BOSU ball, alternating 1 leg standing position, etc. incorporate an incredible level of cerebellar, hippocampal, and frontal lobe activity in order to maintain balance and coordination in such a dynamic environment. A consistent diet of new, unstable, high demand exercises is an incredible super-star supplement for the cerebellum, frontal lobes and hippocampus.

If you consider walking your major form of exercise then throw some dynamic, holistic movements in it.

1. Try stopping every 2 minutes while you walk and do 30 seconds of high knee sprinting in place and slap your opposite hand to opposite knee.

2. Try 30 seconds of stepping with one leg and punching forward and across your body with the other arm. Step with left leg and punch across with right arm and then do the opposite.

3. Spend time walking backwards, side-to-side and doing karaoke type dance moves to get full rotation into the hips. This trains the body in all three planes and fires off many more neuronal networks than traditional walking.

If you are already exercising regularly be sure to incorporate core stability work, surge training and resistance training into your schedule. You will also want to work on your balance by utilizing stability balls, doing one legged exercises, movements with your eyes closed, etc.

## Benefits of Brain-Based Exercise:

1) Improved coordination, balance and skill

2) Improved memory recall and speed of transmission

3) Improved learning skills Improved emotional balance and control

4) Improved focus and determination

5) Improved blood flow to the brain, increasing neuronal metabolism and neurotransmitter formation thus anti-depressant effects (increased serotonin)

6) Increased feelings of joy and euphoria

*For Specifics on Brain Based Exercises go to DrJockers.com where you will find helpful videos and articles.

## Surge Training Boosts Your Brain Better Than Aerobic Exercise

A surge refers to an activity or event that is quick and of high intensity. A glacier surge is a short-lived event where a glacier can move up to velocities 100 times faster than normal. An electrical surge is a very short but intense spike in voltage. Surge training is a new form of exercise that refers to a high-intensity spike in energy output for a short period of time. Research has shown that this form of exercise boosts metabolism and reverses aging more effectively than any other form of exercise or body movement.

Our body is designed to adapt to the ever-changing demands of nature. Exercise enhances our metabolic rate and dramatically increases oxidative stress levels in our body. In response, the body builds up its anti-oxidant reserves in order to successfully adapt to the greater level of stress.

## Surge Training Builds and Protects Your Brain

Two particularly dangerous metabolic byproducts include the hydroxyl free radical and malondialdehyde (MDA). The hydroxyl free radical is highly reactive and is produced in abundant amounts when the body is under stress. When hydroxyl free radicals interact with cell membranes they cause lipid peroxidation. This produces highly reactive cross-linking agents such as MDA that further damage cellular components leading to accelerated aging.

The end product of the damage MDA produces in the body is a pigment called ceroid lipofuscin. This is a product of oxidized cell membranes and mitochondrial membranes. These pigments appear as "age spots," or "liver spots," on the skin of our hands and face. They are a sign of excessive oxidative stress and are associated with accelerated brain degenerative states.

## Surge Training is an Anti-Oxidant

A recent study in rejuvenation research demonstrated the effects of high intensity exercise training. The study looked at 6 individuals exercising at several different intensities. When the subjects exercised at a higher intensity level they had a greater anti-oxidant effect. Additionally, the study showed that each participant produced less hydroxyl free radicals at a higher intensity than at a lower intensity.

## Surge Training Boosts Glutathione

Another recent study published in the Journal of Strength & Conditioning showed that high intensity resistance training decreased MDA and increased glutathione content. Glutathione is the major antioxidant that our cells produce. Higher levels of glutathione are associated with great health and anti-aging effects on the body.

Higher intensity exercise maximizes the body's anaerobic exercise system. The anaerobic system produces lactic acid due to the lowered oxygen state. Most people associate lactic acid with the burn they feel when they exercise. The greater the intensity of exercise = the greater the lactic acid secretion. Researchers now believe that lactic acid may actually act as a free radical scavenger.

High intensity exercise also enhances certain critical enzymes that produce glutathione. This is a natural adaptation the body makes due to the higher free radical load. The combination of increased glutathione and lactate gives high intensity exercise an incredibly powerful anti-oxidant and anti-aging effect.

Surge training utilizes the principles of very high intensity anaerobic exercise for short spurts of time. This style of exercise produces large amounts of lactic acid. A consistent training program challenges the body to become more effective at buffering acidity and free radicals in the system. This bodily adaptation lessens the burden of oxidative stress and allows us to age with grace and beauty.

## Surge Training Tips

1. Warm-up for 5 minutes at a lower intensity

2. Do speed drills where you run (or cycle/elliptical/etc.) for 30 seconds and walk for 30 seconds for 5-10 minutes and then cool down for 5 minutes.

3. Perform high intensity resistance training exercises as described on DrJockers.com

4. Aim to surge train 2-3x each week and do resistance training 2-3x each week.

For More Information on Surge Training go to DrJockers.com

# Chapter Eight

# SuperCharged Mindset

**You are a Champion!**
We have been granted free will by God to perceive life in whatever way we choose. Some use this gift of free will to bless their lives while others use it to curse themselves. Under every circumstance you have a choice on how to think, perceive and react to the situation. You can disempower yourself by thinking like a victim or empower yourself by thinking like a champion.

Victims see many or most of their life circumstances in a negative light. They often point fingers at others and find people, groups and other situations to blame for their challenges. This mentality is extremely disempowering and steals energy from our body.

## Champions Grow From Their Challenges

Champions choose to see life in a completely different perspective. They look at every life challenge as a resistive force to help strengthen their faith, patience and perseverance. Just as a muscle in the body needs resistance to get stronger…our faith needs challenges to grow.

Champions refuse to allow outside circumstances to break them. These people are emotionally mature and have built-up an internal fortitude to step up to the challenges of life. By maintaining integrity and strong values they push into the resistance that life throws at them. As a result, they walk away with deeper life enrichment, knowledge, wisdom and faith. These challenging circumstances provide more opportunity for champions to supercharge their mindset than if they had a comfortable ride through life.

"Consider it all joy, my brethren, when you encounter various trials, knowing that the testing of your faith produces endurance. And let endurance have its perfect result, so that you may be perfect and complete, lacking in nothing." James 1: 2-4

Champions know their identity in God. They know they were called for an amazing purpose on Earth to carry out God's divine plan. They realize that every circumstance offers unique and creative blessings no matter the scenario. Because they live with faith and expectancy they find hidden diamonds at every turn. Even when the world seems to be winning the battle…champions refuse to let up. They maintain a positive attitude and they firmly and consistently remind God and themselves of the divine promises in store for them.

## SuperCharged Awareness

Most people revert into a form of victimhood without even knowing it. Victims do not take personal responsibility but instead look outside of themselves for the cause and solution to their problems. This ultimately leads them to disillusionment and disempowerment. It is only when we have the courage to look within and change and grow ourselves that we are truly empowered.

The following are ways to know that you are slipping into a pattern of victimhood:

> Do you blame outside circumstances such as the economy, the traffic, your co-workers, spouse, kids, etc. for your unhappiness or success?
>
> Do you consistently get frustrated with the people and/or circumstances around you?
>
> Are you depressed or have consistent mood swings?
>
> Do you often feel depressed, irritated, disappointed, etc.?
>
> Do you find that many of your conversations include complaining about outside circumstances and situations?
>
> Do you regularly engage in gossip or negative talk about others?

Do you talk about how you do not enjoy your boss, your car, your job, your spouse, etc?

If you have noticed yourself taking on these attitudes and actions then you have been falling into victimhood and losing your supercharged edge. Gossip and negative talk are disastrous for an individual's health mind, body and spirit.

**Matthew 13:15-17**: "For this people's heart has become calloused; they hardly hear with their ears, and they have closed their eyes. Otherwise they might see with their eyes, hear with their ears, understand with their hearts and turn, and I would heal them. But blessed are your eyes because they see, and your ears because they hear."

I believe Jesus is referring to people who are living in pride and victimhood as having their eyes closed. They have unique circumstances in front of them that would allow them to grow in faith and move closer to Him...but they instead complain or lose interest.

Champions have their eyes open and their ears open to hear the subtle cues and blessings that every circumstance and situation brings into their life. The struggles they encounter allow them to exercise their faith muscles and experience the true richness of life. The invaluable result is that they come to know their God given purpose at a deep and intimate level.

## Steps to Regain Your SuperCharged Edge

You must take personal responsibility for all circumstances and situations in your life. Your mindset must see gratitude and blessing as a way of life. Focusing on gratitude, love & blessing naturally supercharges your energy and life. By keeping your mind on these attitudes regardless of the circumstances you will maintain your supercharged edge and make the most out of the situation.

**Key Belief Systems to Apply**: These are powerful distinctions that you must speak out to nullify the desire to fall back into victimhood. Speaking these declarations over your life creates a wave of physiological momentum that charges you up and increases clean energy. This begins the process of rewiring your neurology…but it takes authentic passion and consistency.

Over time, these powerful declarations are on the forefront of your mind and they BECOME THE ANSWER to every challenging circumstance and situation you encounter. This is an exhilarating feeling to have the word of God on the forefront of your mind. It gives you the freedom to live life boldly and audaciously knowing that you are equipped to grow from any challenge that comes your way.

## Here are some examples of SuperCharged Energy Statements

*"I have complete security because I see myself the way God sees me…as His son/daughter as an heir to the throne of the Kingdom of Heaven."*

*"I know that God has amazing blessings in store for me despite these circumstances."*

*"I have the wisdom of the Lord concerning every decision I make"*

*"I am fully resourced to do everything God has called me to do"*

*"I was born to rise above this adversity and to triumph in the face of defeat"*

Speaking and living out these powerful declarations is life changing. It pulls one out of victimhood and into the noble walk of a champion as God intended for us. Make a daily habit out of speaking bold, audacious faith statements over your life. Do it proactively, not just in a reactive crisis management oriented fashion. Over time, these statements become who you are. When you take on your royal identity you rise up to be the true champion God created you to be.

# Chapter Nine

# SuperCharged Brain Strategies

When you are feeling mentally sluggish try applying some of the following strategies.

1. **Drink Water with Lemon:** The food and beverages we eat provide electrically charged molecules that initiate energy production in our body. Clean water and lemon is the most electrically active thing you could put in your body.

   Clean water with lemon provides the body with hydration, anti-oxidants and electrolytes. Lemon is a rich source of the immune boosting vitamin C. It also has good quantities of electrolytes such as potassium, calcium and magnesium. Lemon is a tremendous source of citrus bioflavonoid anti-oxidant phytonutrients that have been given the label Vitamin P. These nutrients charge your brain up!

2. **Take a Smell of Your Favorite Essential Oil:** Essential oils have been used for thousands of years for their healing and purifying effects on the body. There are 188 references to these precious oils in the Bible. They have always held extreme value by ancient doctors and medicine men that used them for aromatherapy, consumption, and skin application. Research has now revealed the remarkable healing properties within these essential oils.

   Some favorites include citrus essential oils, peppermint, clove and cinnamon. Put a drop on your hands and mix together and then cover your nose and inhale the healing vapors. This will stimulate your brain and increase blood flow to your cranium.

3. **Do a Quick Surge of Exercise:** A quick surge of exercise for 30-60 seconds will get you breathing heavy and enhance blood flow to your brain that will sustain for at least 30 minutes. Try running in place or doing jumping jacks as fast as you can for 30 seconds.

You could also try doing a cross crawl where you take your right hand touch your left thigh and then the left hand to your right thigh during the running process. This will enhance the synchronization between the two hemispheres of your brain.

4. **Snack on Rosemary or Fennel Seeds:** These are a concentrated form of minerals like calcium, potassium, manganese, magnesium, selenium, zinc, copper, & iron. These nutrients along with the strong flavor will stimulate your brain and improve memory and cognitive processing.

Fennel seeds increase circulation to the brain, neutralize acids, aid in digestion and are an incredibly good breath freshener. This is perfect when you are in a hurry, on the road, or eating out at restaurants. Simply put a small container of fennel seeds in your purse or car and pop these seeds throughout the day to keep your breath fresh and your saliva alkaline.

5. **Use a Wobble Board:** Wobble board and wobble disc exercises help to restore and reinforce healthy sacral movement and initiate the CerebroSpinal Fluid (CSF) pump. The CSF brings oxygen and nutrients up into the brain. This has a powerful effect on memory formation and keeping the brain functioning high and empowered to be creative.

The wobble board has a very small center of gravity that creates a greater challenge to the coordinating centers of the brain. Simply sit on the wobble disc and move the body with the pelvis and torso moving in opposite directions. Do front and back exercises and side to side exercises on the narrow pivot of the wobble disc.

6. **Sit Tall and Breathe Deeply:** Effective and efficient oxygenation of the cells, tissues, and organs of our body is an absolute energy necessity. Our respiration cycles are governed by the autonomic nervous system. When your body is under stress you tend to take short, shallow breaths. Because these breaths only penetrate into the upper portion of the chest and lungs they are called "chest breaths."

Several studies have shown that heart disease, depression, anxiety and chronic pain patients have an intimate relationship with persistent shallow, chest breathing behaviors. Several researchers have suggested maintenance of posture and breathing habits to be the most important factor in health and energy promotion.

Sit tall and take 5-10 long deep breaths. You should aim for a 5-10 second inhalation process and a 5-10 second exhalation process. This is a full, deep respiration and brings tons of oxygen into the brain and strips out carbon dioxide and other wastes.

7. **Take a Barefoot Walk Outside:** The Earth's electrical rhythms play a significant role in the natural circadian rhythms that govern our sleep/wake cycle, hormones, mood and energy production. Studies taken on people fully disconnected from this natural electrical rhythm have shown abnormal circulating cortisol levels indicating abnormal stress responses. Additionally, disconnected people often struggle with issues such as insomnia, brain fog, hormone disruption, chronic pain, headaches and fatigue among other things.

The human body has a very similar makeup to the Earth being they are both a combination of water and minerals. This combination is what conducts electrical currents. Our bodies were made to be connected with the Earth and this subtle electrical energy has extremely powerful effects on our health and well-being.

## Earthing Basics

Avoid wearing shoes whenever possible

Sit outside barefoot with your feet on grass or soil.

Walk or run barefoot outside on grass, sand or soil. Moist ground or grass is the perfect electrical conductor.

Expose any part of the body to the Earth, ground or any natural waters like lakes, streams or oceans. Walking in salt water is one of the best grounding techniques due to the combination of earth, water and electrolytes.

Sit or lean on the trunk or limb of a tree to share some of its natural electricity.

Try to incorporate as much sunshine on major regions of your body when you are outside as well to get electrical energy and vitamin D3 synthesis.

The benefits of Earthing (also called grounding) include reduced inflammation and better internal stress management. This results in better sleep, enhanced immunity, less pain and a better state of mind. Many individuals report significantly better memory, creativity, innovativeness and spiritual direction after spending time connecting with the Earth.

8. **Take a Cold Shower:** Cold showers or alternating shower temperatures between warm and cold has a powerful effect on circulation. When you expose yourself to cold temperatures your body constricts blood supply. When exposed to heat the vessels dilate and expand. Changing these temperatures and particularly using cold water dramatically improves the tone of the blood vessel walls. This gives the body a greater adaptability in driving blood into areas that are needed.

Research has indicated that taking cold showers releases endorphins and improves circulation throughout the body including the brain. The net effect of this is that cold showers have been shown to help individuals suffering with depression, insomnia, anxiety and mental lethargy.

The best strategy for beginning to use cold shower therapy is to begin with a comfortable warm shower and then switch the temperature lower towards the end of the shower. If you do this consistently, over time your body will adapt and get more tolerant with the temperature change and you will reap the health benefits.

9. **Take a Power Nap:** Most of us remember nap times when we were children. Sleep researchers have found that napping is actually one of the best ways to boost athletic performance and learning skills. It is estimated now that over 70% of American society is suffering symptoms related to sleep deprivation. Napping is an ideal tool to be used by anyone from athlete to lay person looking to improve performance and quality of life.

Napping has been shown to help consolidate memory. Even short power naps have been shown to improve the immune system and reduce inflammation. This allows for better neurological communication and improved brain function.

Most experts agree that the optimal time period for a nap is between 10 and 30 minutes. This period brings the best rejuvinatory benefit without creating excess sleepiness and effecting nighttime sleep. Even a short 5 minute nap has shown to be beneficial on human performance.

10. **Snack on Raw Cacao:** As described earlier in the book cacao contains theobromine which is a natural cardiovascular stimulant that enhances blood flow to the brain. Theobromine is both safe and non-addictive and has shown clinical benefits with improved memory and cognitive processing.

You can munch on some raw cacao nibs or make a low-sugar shake or pudding with raw cacao to get a good load of this superfood in a very tasty manner. See the SuperCharged Recipe Guide and DrJockers.com for some great cacao based recipes.

## Three Broader Lifestyle Strategies to Incorporate

The following three strategies will not necessarily boost your brain function immediately but incorporated into a regular lifestyle they will help you significantly improve your cognitive acceleration, memory and mood.

# Sun Charge Your Brain

Researchers believe that vitamin D3 acts to protect an aging brain and boost overall memory and cognitive function. This is thought to be done by increasing levels of protective antioxidants, increasing key hormones and suppressing a hyperactive immune system that can inflame the neurological circuitry. Sun charge your brain for maximal cognitive function.

The sun provides our body with an essential stress through its UV radiation. This UV radiation signals a molecule on the skin (7-dehydrocholesterol) to convert to the active form of Vitamin D3 (cholecalciferol) in the body.

## Vitamin D is more Hormone than Vitamin

Vitamin D more resembles a hormone than vitamin by function. Hormones are chemical messengers that interact with cell receptors to produce specific biological responses. Calcitriol, the active form of Vitamin D, is arguably the most powerful hormone in the body. It has the ability to activate over 2,000 genes (roughly 10% of the human genome).

There are vitamin D receptors throughout the central nervous system and critical regions of the brain including the hippocampus. Researchers have concluded that vitamin D activates and deactivates enzymes in the brain and cerebrospinal fluid that are involved in nerve growth, synaptic density and neurotransmitter synthesis.

Vitamin D3 is also shown to boost glutathione production in the neuronal cells protecting them from damage inflicted by oxidative stress. Vitamin D also helps to modulate the immune system to reduce inflammation throughout the body.

## Vitamin D Boosts Cognitive Acceleration

A 2009 study led by scientists at the University of Manchester in England, looked at vitamin D levels and cognitive performance in more than 3,100 men aged 40 to 79 in eight different countries across Europe. The data shows that those people with lower vitamin D levels exhibited slower cognitive processing speed.

Vitamin D deficiency is a current epidemic in our society today affecting 90% of our world's population. According to Vitamin D expert Michael Holick, "We estimate that vitamin D deficiency is the most common medical condition in the world." It is clear that most people are not getting enough healthy sun exposure.

## Vitamin D Deficiencies Increase Brain Degenerative Processes

A 2010 study published in the Archives of Internal Medicine showed that those who are classified as deficient in vitamin D were 42% more likely to have cognitive impairment. Meanwhile, those classified as severely deficient were almost 400% more likely of having cognitive impairment.

"The odds of cognitive impairment increase as vitamin D levels go down," says study author David Llewellyn. "Given that both vitamin D deficiency and dementia are common throughout the world this is a major public health concern."

## Sun Exposure and Vitamin D Production

The ideal amount of sun exposure should produce somewhere in the range of 10,000 – 20,000 IU of vitamin D3. This depends upon the amount of body parts exposed, the strength or angle of the sun and the color of the individual's skin.

This is the approximate amount of time each individual skin type needs of sun exposure to get the appropriate 10,000 – 20,000 IU considering that at least 60% of the body is exposed to sunlight. This would be equivalent to intentionally sun bathing. They should get this amount at least three times weekly in order to fully optimize vitamin D3 levels.

1. Light skin = 15-20 minutes daily
   Medium Skin = 25-30 minutes daily
   Dark Skin = 40-45 minutes daily

2. Use coconut oil, aloe vera and/or green tea extract as a moisturizer before and after sun exposure for added anti-oxidant protection

3. If adequate sunlight is not available or attainable than supplement with 8,000-10,000 IU of vitamin D3 daily

## Listen to Some Good Music

Most people have their own particular styles of music they enjoy. Music is one of the greatest joys of mankind and it has an effect at simulating the brain and enhancing learning. Listening to music stimulates the whole brain through diverse neural circuitry which increases cranial metabolism. Listening to enjoyable music improves your brain function.

The brain is divided into two major hemispheres called the right and left hemisphere. The right brain is thought to process information through creative imagery. The left brain is the analytical side that controls verbal and mathematical processing. The corpus callosum connects the left and right hemispheres and controls the communication between these two.

## Music Helps Connect Your Brain Hemispheres

Music is unique in that it activates a broad array of neurons across the corpus callosum. This creates a state of harmony between the two hemispheres. The non-verbal melodies of music stimulate the right brain while singing stimulates the language center in the left hemisphere.

Music has the amazing potential to alter an individual's state of consciousness. Music therapy has been shown to shift a person's complete perception of time and stimulates unique emotions and memories. Listening to music boosts endorphin release which lifts our spirits and activates positive emotions and states of euphoria.

## Music Helps Boost Creative Energies

Music also boosts creative energies through the production of alpha and theta waves. Large influxes of alpha waves induce states of enhanced creativity while theta waves are associated with dreaming, learning and relaxing.

The key for boosting creative energies is to listen to the type of music you enjoy the most. If you want more inspiration in language and mathematics it would make sense to listen to music with singing while music without words stimulates more artistic and visual senses.

These types of music can also be used to help balance the hemispheres effectively. Someone who has a left brain focused job such as an accountant may experience an increased level of peace and stability when they listen to classical music or other right brain style music.

Someone with a heavy right brain position (such as an artist) may do well with rock 'n roll or other lyric based music to charge up their left brain. This is all subjective to the unique tendencies and subtleties of the individual but more research is pointing in the direction of using music to balance and stabilize the hemispheres.

## The Right Type of Music

I personally prefer inspirational music that is only instrumental for relaxation and worship music when I want to supercharge my energy! I believe these forms of music are divinely inspired and lift our spirits better than any other form of music. Music with immoral or depressing lyrics is poison to the spirit and I highly recommend avoiding this form of music.

## Music Therapy and Your Health

Classical or light music help to calm and relax blood pressure. Researchers have shown that listening to calming music for periods of time every day is extremely effective for stabilizing blood pressure levels.

Music therapy is used to help patients with neurological conditions by stimulating unique regions and enhancing blood flow and metabolism. This sort of therapy was popularized by Dr. Oliver Sacks and featured in the movie "Awakenings."

## Music Therapy and Alzheimer's Disease

Alzheimer's disease is associated with damage to the temporal lobe that is used to process and direct memories. Music stimulates not only direct memories but other circumstances surrounding that musical experience. Researchers have found that listening to music can indirectly stimulate memory fragments that would not otherwise be retrieved. This helps to provide emotional comfort and improve brain function.

## Music Therapy and Parkinson's Disease

Parkinson's disease is a pathogenic process that destroys the basal ganglia. This region of the brain organizes thoughts and movements into action. Strong, rhythmic musical beats stimulate motor control, movement and coordination. Combining this music with dance steps and other movements has been shown to improve walking speed and coordination for individuals with Parkinson's.

## Fasting Improves Your Brain Function

New research has indicated that fasting can significantly reduce the effects of aging on the brain. It has been known that bouts of intermittent fasting have a powerful anti-inflammatory effect on the entire body. Leading scientists now believe that intermittent fasting is one of the key strategies for maximizing brain function.

Researchers at the National Institute of Aging in Baltimore have reviewed the literature and performed studies to indicate the positive effects of fasting on overall brain health. Professor Mark Mattson, who is the head of the Institute's laboratory of NeuroSciences, made it clear that these benefits were not just related to calorie restriction but instead to intentional periods of intermittent fasting.

## Major Physiological Phases
## Building and Cleansing

Eating stimulates the body to go into building phase where we are anabolic in nature and store both nutrients and toxins. This phase is essential for building new cells and tissues and store nutrients for times of scarcity. This building phase of physiology is predominately led by the hormone insulin.

Fasting for more than four hours begins the cleansing phase. The cleansing phase is catabolic in nature in that it tears down old damaged cells. This process turns on brain autophagy, or "self-eating," in where the cells recycle waste material, regulate waste products and repair themselves. These genetic repair mechanisms are turned on through the release of human growth hormone (HGH).

Intermittent fasting is one of the most powerful modalities for reducing inflammation, boosting immunity and enhancing tissue healing. This is one of the reasons why many people feel nauseated when they have infections. This innate mechanism is the body's way of influencing us to fast so it can produce the right environment to boost natural immunity.

## Fasting Boosts Human Growth Hormone (HGH)

HGH is known to create physiological changes in metabolism to favor fat burning and protein sparing. The proteins and amino acids are utilized to improve brain and neuron processing. They also repair tissue collagen which improves the functionality and strength of muscles, tendons, ligaments, and bones. HGH also improves skin function, reduces wrinkles and heals cuts and burns faster.

Researchers at the Intermountain Medical Center Heart Institute found that men, who had fasted for 24 hours, had a 2000% increase in circulating HGH. Women who were tested had a 1300% increase in HGH. The researchers found that the fasting individuals had significantly reduced their triglycerides, boosted their HDL cholesterol and stabilized their blood sugar.

## The Dance Between Insulin and HGH to Govern Metabolism

HGH and insulin are opposites in function. HGH is focused on tissue repair, efficient fuel usage and anti-inflammatory immune activity. Insulin is designed for energy storage, cellular division and pro-inflammatory immune activity.

Insulin is the dominant player in this game. When conditions demand an insulin release (carbohydrate intake), HGH is inhibited. Additionally, too much protein or fat may not stimulate insulin but they will inhibit HGH release.

Studies have indicated that the disruption of neuronal autophagy results in accelerated neurodegenerative states throughout the brain. Elevated circulating levels of insulin reduce the amount of neuronal autophagy and cause metabolic problems as well as accelerated degenerative states. Bouts of intermittent fasting are essential for the brain to clean itself up and drive new neurons and communication lines for optimal function.

## Fasting and Exercise

The cleansing phase also acts like a slinky that is being spring-loaded for when the body moves into the building stage. It provides a sort of pre-load that allows the body to adapt in an incredible manner when it goes into the building phase. This enhances the neuronal connections and improves brain function.

Experts believe the intermittent fasting puts the brain cells under mild stress that is similar to the effects of exercise on muscle cells. The stress causes them to adapt and get more energy efficient. The body recovers from intense exercise through both the building and cleansing phases.

## Fasting Boosts Brain-Derived NeuroTrophic Factor (BDNF)

BDNF levels govern the formation of new neurons and the development of synapses and various lines of communication within the brain. Higher levels of BDNF lead to healthier neurons and better communication processes between these neurological cells. Low levels of BDNF are linked to dementia, Alzheimer's, memory loss and other brain processing problems.

Research has shown that bouts of fasting have a great anti-inflammatory effect on the entire body. Sufferers from asthma have shown great results as have preliminary reports on individuals with Alzheimer's and Parkinson's. Mattson and colleagues are preparing to study more details about the impact of fasting on the brain using MRI technology and other testing.

## Best Strategies for Fasting

The best way to begin fasting is by giving your body 12 hours between dinner and breakfast every single day. This allows 4 hours to complete digestion and 8 hours for the liver to complete its detoxification cycle. After this is a standard part of lifestyle, try taking one day a week and extending the fast to 16-18 hours. Eventually, you may choose to do a full 24 hour fast each week.

During the Fasting Period it is great to drink cleansing beverages such as fermented drinks, herbal teas, water with infused superfood extracts, water with lemon or apple cider vinegar, etc. These enhance the cleansing process by providing anti-oxidants and micronutrients that enhance healing while not interacting with insulin or HGH levels.

## Precautionary Step Before Fasting

Before one begins a lifestyle of intermittent fasting they should first remove as much sugar and grains from their diet as possible.

This will create better blood sugar balance and help regulate insulin and the stress hormone cortisol. The diet should be built around good fats, anti-oxidants, clean protein and fiber. It can take three to seven days to stabilize blood sugar and stress hormones before intermittent fasting would be advised.

Once the body is properly trained, most people are able to easily do a 16-18 hour fast every day. The easiest way to do this is by missing breakfast to extend the overnight fast. I do this every day myself. In the morning time, I drink lots of water and utilize anti-oxidant extracts in the form of herbal teas, water infusions and fresh squeezed lemon, fermented herbal botanicals and apple cider vinegar. These cleansing beverages help to detoxify the body and enhance healing processes. They also quell hunger and keep your energy levels high.

I have a light lunch or mid-afternoon snack that is either a big raw salad with good fats like olive oil and avocado or a protein shake with non-denatured whey, coconut and avocado. At night I have a large dinner with lots of grass-fed beef or another animal protein/fat and tons of veggies.

For many people, such as myself, we feel so great on an intermittent fasting lifestyle that we choose to never go back to eating any differently. In fact, I love to combine this fasting lifestyle with bouts of surge training to maximize my HGH levels and brain boosting strategies!

# Chapter Ten

# Brain Boosting Supplements

The brain depends upon specific nutrients in order to function with peak capacity. There are certain nutrients that are challenging to get from our diet and lifestyles. These nutrients can be supplemented with whole food based sources. These are some of the most specific nutritional supplements for healthy brain function.

**Vitamin D3:**

This is extremely critical for brain development and maturity throughout life. Lowered Vitamin D3 levels are associated with autism, dyslexia and ADHD in children and neurodegenerative diseases like MS, ALS, dementia, Alzheimer's & Parkinson's in adults.

The optimal source of vitamin D3 is through the sun. Most of our ancestors were able to derive optimal vitamin D3 levels through regular sun exposure. In the Northern climates, they would get a lot in the summer and then their diet of fatty fish, mushrooms and raw milk that naturally contain little bits of D3 would keep them going in the winter.

Researchers have found that the optimal vitamin D3 levels are between 70-100ng/ml. Over 95% of society is are under these levels. Taking 10,000 IU of vitamin D3 (2,000IU for infants and small children and 5,000 IU for those under 120lbs) daily is a great way to ensure your levels are optimized and your brain development is at its peak.

## Omega-3 Fatty Acids:

Omega 3 fatty acids help to reduce neurological inflammation and improve brain function. Omega 3's help provide better cell membrane receptor activity and are key players in the development of the brain and the formation of neurotransmitters.

Omega 3's help protect the brain and eyes from inflammatory damage and reduces the risk for blindness, cataracts, macular degeneration, dementia, Alzheimer's Disease and other neurological disorders.

Take 1-2 grams of EPA/DHA daily for optimal brain health. I recommend a purified fish oil form with added gamma-linoleic acid (GLA) in a dose of about 150-300 mg.

## Probiotics:

Gut health is extremely critical to brain health. Children with neurodevelopmental problems like Autism, dyslexia and ADHD are known to have leaky gut syndromes and often have very profound food sensitivities.

When the gut is damaged it allows food particles to cross into the blood stream where the immune system creates an inflammatory attack. This inflammation passes into the brain and screws up neurological processing.

Many individuals have dysbiosis or bad bacterial balance in their gut and parasites like Candida. The parasites and opportunistic bacteria release toxins into the blood stream that get into the brain and cause inflammation leading to poor memory, brain fog and advanced states of brain degeneration.

Supplement with a high quality probiotic that has key lactobacillus and bifido bacterium strains and over thirty billion colony forming units. This is the probiotic that will deliver results and you will feel the difference after a week.

# Methylation Support:

Methylation is a key biochemical process that happens billions of times every second to repair the DNA in the body. B vitamins, zinc and magnesium are the key components to healthy methylation processes.

**Magnesium:** Research has shown that magnesium helps to support the blood brain barrier and preventing synapse loss and reversing memory decline in individuals with neurodegenerative diseases.

**B Vitamins:** These all play an important role in the formation of neurotransmitters. Deficiencies in any of the B vitamins can cause serious issues with neurotransmitter formation and balance. Individuals with an MTHFR or MTRR gene polymorphisms are more likely to be deficient in B2, B6, folate and B12 and are at greater risk for the development of cognitive impairment

**Zinc:** This is a key cofactor for dopamine synthesis which is key for healthy mood and concentration levels. Low zinc status depresses serotonin and melatonin production which can affect behavior and sleep. Low zinc levels are associated with ADHD, poor memory, depression and neurodegenerative conditions.

# NeuroTransmitter Support Nutrients:

The body makes key neurotransmitters such as dopamine, serotonin, GABA, acetylcholine and more. Certain nutrients enhance the production and utilization of these neurotransmitters.

**Choline:** This is a key precursor to the neurotransmitter acetylcholine and it helps to regulate memory, focus and muscle control. Choline supplementation improves memory, attention span and cognitive acceleration while preventing neurodegeneration.

**Serine:** Phosphatidylserine (PS) has been shown to increase dopamine levels. Research has shown that taking PS improved both memory, behavior and hyperactivity in kids diagnosed with ADHD.

## Mitochondrial Support Nutrients:

Every cell of the body has mitochondria within it that produce energy for the cell. The mitochondria are the battery packs of the cell and they are extremely important.

The more high functioning mitochondria a cell has the more energy it can produce and the better our overall health is. High levels of oxidative stress wear down the mitochondria and cause a dysfunctional state.

**L-Carnitine:** Plays a critical role in fatty acid metabolism and mitochondrial health. It also improves the development and usage of key neurotransmitters norepinephrine and serotonin. These neurotransmitters play an important role in memory, concentration and mood.

**CoQ10:** Coenzyme Q10 is an essential cofactor in the mitochondria of every cell and it is a potent anti-oxidant. Supplementing with CoQ10 has been shown to dramatically improve brain mitochondria. This improves memory and higher cognitive function while preventing against the development of neurodegenerative disease.

**N-Acetyl Cysteine:** This compound provides a key rate limiting factor in glutathione production. Glutathione is our master anti-oxidant and protects brain and neurological tissue from oxidative stress.

Research shows that it improves function in individuals suffering from addiction, depression, compulsive disorders, bipolar, schitzophrenia and neurodegenerative diseases like dementia, Alzheimer's and Parkinson's.

**Alpha Lipoic Acid:** This is a unique and powerful anti-oxidant that has both water and fat soluble properties. This unique characteristic allows it to be absorbed and transported into many organs and systems such as the brain, liver and nerves.

This has been shown to protect against neurodegenerative processes in the brain and is a powerful supplement to support higher cognitive development.

## Brain Health Support Pack:

My Brain Support Pack is designed to get you the key nutrients that are necessary for optimal brain function and cognitive processing.

These nutrients help the brain to produce the right amount of neurotransmitters and other neurochemicals. Additionally, these key nutrients have a powerful effect at reducing the inflammatory fires that destroy our brain tissue.

# Chapter Eleven

# The SuperCharged Lifestyle

Great job finishing this book and learning the best strategies to Supercharge Your Brain! If you begin following and applying the rules and principles outlined in this book I guarantee you will notice significant improvements in your energy levels and mental stamina. You will also be preventing and perhaps reversing brain degenerative processes that would have left you mentally crippled.

So the first step is to get yourself healthy and continue to work on growing and maturing in these strategies. You should never think that you will have it all figured out but instead that you are pressing forward and working to improve your lifestyle each day. Overtime, you will see that you have come a long way.

The next step is to share this message with others. Not just those who are already sick and diseased but those who are closest to you. Social support is a huge part of success in healthy lifestyle pursuits. If your spouse and family are not in agreement or if they are left in the dark about this, it will make the course ten times harder. Do everything you can to get them on board with you.

Keep a copy of this book for you to continually resource but share other copies with those closest to you and those you know who are looking to elevate their life. You never know how far reaching something you think, say or do today will impact the world days, weeks, years and decades from now. God bless you for being a world changer!

To a SuperCharged Life,
Dr. David Jockers

# Chapter Twelve

# SuperCharge Your Brain Recipes

The following recipes are based on the SuperCharge Your Energy nutrition plan that Dr Jockers developed. Each recipe is loaded with brain boosting superfoods. All of these recipes are uniquely named for their ability to improve your brain function & supercharge your life!

These recipes contain none of the most inflammatory and allergenic foods including gluten containing grains, pasteurized dairy, pig, shellfish, soy, tomatoes & peanuts. Organic eggs are included and they are much less allergenic than feed-lot eggs. Raw, grass-fed dairy is included in many recipes because it is a very high quality superfood.

If you have a food sensitivity to grass-fed dairy, eggs, nightshades like tomatoes and bell peppers or any other unique foods found in these recipes than by all means exclude the sensitive foods from the recipes.

For more information on each recipe and to see other superfood recipes, recipe books, articles and videos go to DrJockers.com

# Breakfast/Lunch

## Brain Building Omelet

3 organic range eggs
2 oz. grass-fed cheese
3 tbsp. grass-fed butter/ghee/coconut oil
1/2 cup chopped red onions
8 organic chopped green onions
1 cup chopped organic yellow pepper
6 clove of minced garlic
1 tbsp. organic thyme
1 tbsp. organic oregano
1 tbsp. organic basil
2 tbsp. turmeric

### Directions:

Saute onions, green onions and garlic in pan on a low heat for 10 minutes.
Add in eggs, cheese and herbs.
Cook for 10 minutes and add in turmeric. You will Love This!

## The Big Brain Shake Ingredients:
1 can Coconut Milk or 2 cups of carton coconut milk
Coconut Oil, if necessary if you use the carton milk
½ to 1 cup Blueberries
1 to 2 scoops of Brain SuperCharge Protein Powder
½ tsp Cinnamon
1 tsp Fish Oil

Optional Ingredients:
Organic, Pasture-Raised Eggs
Turmeric
Greens Powder
Flax Seed
Vegetables (spinach, kale, etc)
Probiotic capsule (empty capsule in shake)

## Directions:
Put the eggs, fish oil, & hemp oil (if using) in last in order to limit any damage to the fats and proteins from the blender itself. Put it on a light spin cycle and this will simply mix up all these ingredients.

## Fat Burning Berry Shake Ingredients:

1/3 can of organic full-fat Coconut Milk
1 Scoop of non-denatured vanilla whey protein
1 cup of frozen raspberries or strawberries
1 tsp of Cinnamon
Pinch of Cayenne Pepper
Stevia to taste
Servings: 1-2

## Fat Burning Berry Shake Instructions

Put all the ingredients in together, mix and enjoy!

If you want to use the carton coconut milk, I would suggest adding in 1 tbsp of coconut oil or coconut butter for more coconut fats.

This recipe is full of healthy medium-chain fatty acids that help to produce ketones and move our body into a state of fat-adaption where we are burning fat as our primary fuel. These MCT's also help to improve digestive function, thyroid function, stabilize blood sugar levels and balance overall hormones.

## Blueberry Pudding Ingredients:
2 cups of full-fat organic coconut milk (in can)
3 avocados
1 cup of wild blueberries
4 tbsp. ground chia seed
1 scoop non denatured, grass-fed whey protein
1/2 tsp. pink salt
1 tbsp. of vanilla
5 drops of organic stevia (only if needed)
**Servings:** 4

## Blueberry Pudding Instructions:
Blend all ingredients together in a vita mix or blender.
Refrigerate for 12 hours.
Your pudding is ready!

## Spinach Pancakes Ingredients:
4 organic (pasture-raised) eggs
1/4 cup full-fat organic coconut milk
1/2 tsp. pink salt
2/3 cup frozen organic spinach
2 cloves of garlic
1/2 cup onion chopped
1/3 cup coconut flour
1/2 tsp. baking powder
black pepper to taste
1 tbsp. extra-virgin coconut oil
**Servings:** About 3 pancakes

## Spinach Pancakes Directions:
Blend, eggs, coconut milk or amasai, salt, spinach, garlic and onion together in a blender or vita mix.
Add coconut flour and baking powder and blend.
Melt a tbsp. of coconut oil on medium to low stove.
Drop batter in by heaping tbsp. at a time.
Sprinkle with black pepper.

## BlueBerry Brain Muffins Ingredients:

3 organic eggs
1/2 cup melted coconut oil
1/4 cup Coconut water
2 tbsp. honey
15 drops vanilla cream stevia
1/2 tsp. Pink salt
1/2 cup organic blueberries
1/2 cup coconut flour
3/4 tsp. aluminum-free baking powder

**Servings:** About 4-6 muffins

## BlueBerry Brain Muffins Directions:
Combine, eggs, oil, coconut water, honey, stevia, and pink salt together. Add flour and baking powder and let it thicken for 5 minutes.

Add blueberries and bake at 325 for 15-20 minutes.

## Tomato Basil Big Brain Omelet

1 small organic tomato (chopped)
1 tsp. organic basil
1 tsp. fresh garlic
1 tsp. pink salt
3 organic pasture-raised eggs
1 tbsp. organic coconut oil/ghee/butter (butter/ghee MUST be pasture-raised)

## Instructions:
In a frying pan place oil to melt on medium heat.
Whisk eggs together with basil garlic and salt.
Pour into the pan.
When it is almost cooked add tomatoes to the middle of the eggs.
Flip eggs over to form an omelet.

Serve with organic goat cheese, feta cheese or raw grass-fed cheese

## Chocolate Mint Cereal Bowl Ingredients:

1 can of full-fat coconut milk
6-8 tbsps of chia seeds
1 tbsp of spirulina
Handful of cacao nibs
1 scoop of high quality protein powder
½ tsp of mint or peppermint extract
Splash of vanilla pasture-raised)
Stevia to taste

## Chocolate Mint Cereal Bowl Instructions:

Blend or stir coconut milk, stevia, spirulina, protein powder, mint, vanilla.

Pour into the bowl or container you are going to store it in.
Stir in chia seeds and let sit in fridge for 20-30 minutes.

This is a completely grain-free, low carb cereal that tastes amazing! This cereal bowl is perfect to enjoy for a dessert or breakfast and you can change it up in so many different ways!.

# Side Dishes:

## Coconut Flour Bread Recipe Ingredients:

1 cup of cashew or almond butter
¼ cup of coconut flour
5 pasture-raised eggs
½ tsp of aluminum-free baking powder
½ tsp of baking soda
2 tsp apple cider vinegar
**Optional:** 1 tbsp of raw honey
**Servings: 5**

## Coconut Flour Bread Recipe Instructions:

Pre-heat over to 350 degrees. Gather all ingredients and let sit out at room temperature. Pour into the bowl or container you are going to store it in. **Stir in chia seeds and let sit in fridge for 20-30 minutes.**

Place ingredients into vitamix or blend tech blender. Can also use hand blender or food processor Blend until well combined and smooth. Pour batter into well greased 8.5 x 4 loaf pan.

Bake 25-30 minutes.

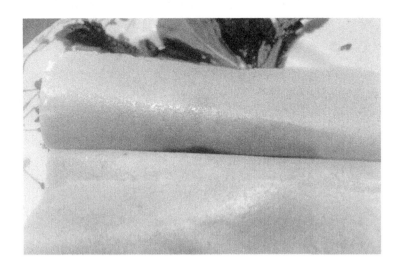

## Guacamole Coconut Wrap Ingredients:
2 Coconut flour wraps

1 handful of green leafy veggies (spinach, collards etc)

2 avocados

1/4 cup of organic coconut milk (carton variety)

1/8 cup of organic apple cider vinegar (ACV)

1/2 organic tomato diced

1/4 red onion diced

Herbs

**Optional Ingredients:**
Free range chicken or grass-fed cheese slices for protein

**Directions:** Mash guacamole and add in coconut milk and ACV and mix together until smooth, creamy and tangy. Add in diced tomatoes and onions and herbs and mix until you get your desired flavor

Add guacamole to coconut wraps (start small as these wraps can't hold a lot of guacamole) and then add your greens.

## Not Nut Butter Ingredients:

3 tbsp. softened coconut butter (raw organic)
2 tbsp. virgin coconut oil (melted is best)
1 scoop of high quality protein powder
½ tsp. real salt
½ tsp. vanilla
Sprinkle of cinnamon (if desired)

## Not Nut Butter Instructions:

Mix all ingredients together.
Serve with celery, flax crackers or other veggies.

This recipe is loaded with good fats, clean proteins, anti-oxidants and enzymes. This digests very well as the vast majority of the fats are from coconut which is full of MCT's which do not depend on bile for breakdown. This is easier on the digestive system than typical nut butters.

## Protein Popping Power Balls Ingredients:

1 cup coconut butter

1 tsp. organic vanilla extract

1 scoop non denatured, grass-fed whey protein

½ cup raw coconut flakes

½ cup of raw chia seed

1 tsp. pink salt

**Servings:** Makes 8 small balls

## Protein Popping Power Balls Instructions:

Mix all the ingredients together and roll into a ball.

The SuperCharged Energy Nutrition plan is based around loading up on healthy fats, anti-oxidants, clean protein, fiber and fermented foods. This recipe has all of these. The good fats come in the form of coconut butter and coconut flakes which have tons of medium chain saturated fats that help us burn fat and balance hormones.

## SuperCharged Chicken Salad Ingredients:

10 oz free range chicken shredded
½ cup vegan mayonnaise (Veganaisse)
1 apple chopped
½ cup raisins
½ cup chopped celery
Sprinkle of nutmeg and cinnamon
Servings: 5


Optional Ingredients:
Italian herbs – basil, oregano, thyme
Diced Cucumber
Diced bell pepper

## SuperCharged Chicken Salad Instructions:

Mix all ingredients until smooth and creamy
Serve on organic romaine lettuce

## Cranial Cauliflower "Rice"

4 heads of organic cauliflower
1 tsp. pink salt
1/2 cup coconut aminos

## Instructions:

With a cheese grater, grate cauliflower.
Mix in salt and coconut aminos and put in a large glass bowl and bake at 350 for 20-30 minutes.

Most of us enjoy the taste of rice, however, rice is an inflammatory food because it metabolizes into glucose and elevates our blood sugar. The result of elevated blood sugar is increased insulin output, advanced glycolytic enzyme (AGE) formation and inflammatory processes.

The SuperCharged Energy Diet recommends going grain and sugar free and this Cranial Cauliflower Rice recipe fits right into this premise. It tastes amazing and is loaded with anti-oxidants and fiber.

# Dinner Recipes

## Brain Boosting Burger

2 pounds of grass-fed beef
2 organic eggs
1/2 cup chia seed blend
1 tbsp. thyme, oregano and basil
2 garlic cloves minced
8 green onions chopped finely
1 tsp. pink salt

## Instructions:
Mix all ingredients together.
Form into patties and cook in coconut oil.

This burger is awesome! It is loaded with essential fats, anti-oxidants, clean proteins & fiber. The brain depends upon a continual supply of saturated fat and omega 3 fatty acids to build healthy neuronal cell membranes. This burger provides those essential fats and is loaded with unique anti-oxidants with the Italian herbs and garlic.

## Super Salmon Burgers

2 large Wild-Alaskan salmon fillets
1/2 cup red onion, chopped finely
1/2 cup fresh organic cilantro, chopped
1/2 cup fresh organic parsley, chopped
4 garlic cloves, minced
2 organic eggs
4 tbsp. chia seeds

**Servings:** 4

**Prep Time:** 10 mins

**Cook Time:** 10 mins

## Instructions:
Peel off the scales of the salmon.
Ground up the fillets in a large bowl and add remaining ingredients.
Form into patties and cook in coconut oil.
Serve with raw veggies and a shot of peppermint terrain

## Tenacious Taco Lettuce Wraps

2 lb. green fed ground beef
2 tbsp. organic no salt seasoning (from costco)
1/4 cup coconut aminos
1 cup shredded really raw cheddar cheese
1 cup Amasai cream cheese
1 cup organic salsa
1 cup chopped red onions
1 cup guacamole
2 heads of organic butterleaf lettuce

## Instructions:

Cook ground beef in coconut oil and add seasoning and coconut aminos.

Once ground beef is done cooking put some in a piece of lettuce and tops with remaining ingredients.

## Anti-Depressant Meatballs

1 lb. green-fed ground beef
1 organic egg
2 tbsp. coconut flour
1 tbsp. basil
1 tbsp. oregano
1 tsp. pink salt

## Instructions:

Mix all ingredients together and form into meatballs
Cook in coconut oil until done
Add sauce and cover to keep warm

## Super Serotonin Sauce

1 can organic tomato paste
1 tbsp. basil
1 tbsp. oregano
1 tsp. pink salt
1/2 cup water
1 glove of garlic minced (optional)

## Instructions:

Mix all ingredients together in a bowl
Pour over meatballs and top with grass-fed raw cheese or goat cheese

## SuperSmart Stir Fry

1 lb. organic 100% green-fed ground beef
2 cups chopped organic broccoli
2 cups chopped organic baby carrots
1 cup organic peas
1 cup organic pea pods
1/2 cup Coconut Aminos (soy sauce replacement)
1-2 tbsp. ginger
1 tsp. pink salt
2 tbsp. coconut oil

## Instructions:
Throw all ingredients into a frying pan and cook!

Asian stir fry's can be the healthiest or the worst thing you consume and it all depends upon the quality of the ingredients. Typical stir fry's that are found in restaurants and frozen dinners are loaded with brain destroying toxins such as unfermented soy, excitotoxins like MSG, preservatives and genetically modified ingredients. This stir fry is loaded with brain boosting fatty acids, anti-oxidants and amino acids.

# Dessert Recipes

## Blueberry Coconut Parfait Ingredients:

1 cup of coconut cream concentrate or coconut butter
1/2 cup of fresh or frozen blueberries
1/2 cup of clean water 6 drops of vanilla stevia (or to your taste)
Pinch of pink salt (Himalayan)
Raspberries or extra blueberries for topping

## Blueberry Coconut Parfait Instructions:

Put blueberries, water, salt and stevia into the blender first, then add the coconut cream or coconut butter and blend. You will need to hand mix with a spoon while the blender is going. This is very challenging on the blender because the coconut cream/butter is so thick. A high quality vita-mix is best for the blending process. Once everything is mixed together, put berries on top and enjoy! You can also put in the freezer for a while and then pull it out and place it in the refrigerator for an hour to thaw out. This is the most popular way to have this as it is cool and tasty!

## Coconut Flour Cookie Ingredient

1 cup of coconut flour
½ cup of grass-fed butter or coconut oil
4 pasture-raised eggs
½ cup of coconut flakes
Pinch of pink salt
1 tsp of vanilla
3 ½ tsps. of raw honey or grade B maple syrup(Low carb) –
1 – 2 tsps of liquid stevia to taste
½ – 1 cup of organic unsweetened chocolate chips

## Coconut Flour Cookie Instructions:

Preheat the oven to 375 degrees.

Melt the honey or syrup and butter together in a small pot.In a large bowl mix together the butter, raw honey or syrup, eggs, vanilla extract and sea salt.Stir in the coconut flour, shredded coconut and chocolate chips.

Line a baking sheet with parchment paper and form batter into bite size balls- just press together in your hands or scoop and press and shape into whatever you shape or size you would like

Bake for 12-15 or until golden brown.

## Chocolate Chia Protein Bites Ingredients:

2 tbsps of almond butter
2 ½ tbsps of raw honey
1 tbsp of coconut oil
1 scoop of high quality protein powder
5 tbsps of raw cacao powder
Pinch of Himalyan pink salt
1-2 tbsps of chia seeds

## Chocolate Chia Protein Bites Instructions:

Gather ingredients and place into a blender or a bowl.Blend or mix by hand until smooth.Batter will be a little sticky and oily.Scoop batter into bit size balls/cookies and place onto a non-stick surface.Eat right away or store in refrigerator.

The combination of good fats in the coconut oil, raw chocolate and chia seeds is a match made in heaven! This recipe will help you burn fat, build healthy lean body tissue, improve digestive function and supercharge your brain!

## Chocolate Goji Bark Ingredients:

2 cups of 75% organic raw dark chocolate

1/4 cup organic raw coconut oil

1/2 cup raw organic goji berries

1/2 cup raw sprouted nuts of your choice (pecans, almonds, macadamia, cashews or pistachios)

Sprinkle of coarse pink Himalayan salt

**Servings:** About 8-10

## Chocolate Goji Bark Instructions:

Melt chocolate and coconut oil together in small pot over low heat until completely melted down. Spread parchment paper over cookie sheet.

Pour chocolate onto parchment. Sprinkle nuts, berries and salt over. Freeze for 30 minutes. Break into pieces and eat.

What a great superfood combination! The synergy between dark chocolate, coconut oil and goji berries is extraordinary. This recipe helps boost dopamine and improve mental clarity and performance.

## Blueberry Coconut Cookies Ingredients

2 cups of shredded coconut flakes
½ cup of virgin coconut oil
1 cup of organic blueberries
3 tbsps of raw honey
½ tsp of vanilla
Pinch of pink salt
**Optional Ingredients:** Liquid stevia to taste instead of honey
**Servings:** 7

## Blueberry Coconut Cookies Instructions

Place all ingredients into blender or a food processor. Process the ingredients for 2-3 minutes until the shredded coconut beings to break down. Drop the batter, about 2-3 teaspoons worth onto a lined cookie sheet. I used my small cookie scoop.

Place in the fridge or freezer to harden for 10-20 minutes. Store in an airtight container in the fridge or freezer.

## SuperGreen Fudge Cups Ingredients:

1 cup coconut oil (soft, not melted)
2/3 cup coconut butter
2/3 cup raw almond butter
1/4 cup raw honey
1/4 cup super-greens powder
1/2 cup raw cacao powder
25 drops vanilla cream stevia
1 tbsp. organic vanilla extract
1/2 cup coconut flakes
1/2 cup slivered almonds
Sprinkle of real salt (for on top)

**Servings:** 8-12 fudge cups

## SuperGreen Fudge Cups Instructions:

Mix all ingredients together. Spoon into muffin tin lined with muffin cups. Sprinkle salt on top and freeze in freezer for 30 minutes.

# Supercharge Your Brain Background Research

## Brain Boosting nutrients

1. Glutathione: new research reveals new benefits. Precursors may be key to restoring health. Focus from Nutricology. July 2008.
2. Monograph: Glutathione, reduced (GSH). Alternative Medicine Review. 6(6), 2001
3. James, S. J., et al. Metabolic biomarkers of increased oxidative stress and impaired methylation capacity in children with autism. American Journal of Clinical Nutrition. 80(6):1611-1617, 2004.
4. Di Monte, D. A., et al. Glutathione in Parkinson's disease: a link between oxidative stress and mitochondrial damage? Ann Neurol. 32(Supplement):S111--S115, 1992.
5. Christen, Y. Oxidative stress and Alzheimer's disease. American Journal of Clinical Nutrition. 71(2):621S-629S, 2000.
6. Jaendel, C., et al. Lipid peroxidation and free radical scavengers in Alzheimer's disease. Gerontology. 35(5-6):275-282, 1989.
7. Knight, J. A. Reactive oxygen species and the neurodegenerative disorders. Annals of Clinical and Laboratory Science (USA). 27(1):11-25, 1997.
8. Packer, L. Antioxidant supplementation affects indices of muscle trauma and oxidant stress in human blood during exercise. Med Sci Sports Exerc. 21(2):42-47, 1989.
9. Mehler, A. H. Amino acid metabolism I: General pathways. In: Devlin, T. M. (editor), Textbook of Biochemistry - With Clinical Correlations (2nd edition). John Wiley & Sons, New York, USA, 1986:483.
10. Sechi, G., et al. Reduced intravenous glutathione in the treatment of early Parkinson's disease. Prog Neuropsychopharmacol Biol Psychiatry. 20(7):1159-1170, 1996.
11. Spina, M. B., et al. Dopamine turnover and glutathione oxidation: implications for Parkinson disease. Proc National Academy of Sciences, USA. 86(4):1398-1400, 1989.
12. Altschule, M. D., et al. Blood glutathione level in mental disease before and after treatment. Arch Psych. 71:69, 1955.
13. Berk, M., et al. N-acetyl cysteine as a glutathione precursor for schizophrenia - a double-blind, randomized, placebo-controlled trial. Biol Psychiatry. 64(5):361-368, 2008.
14. Bounous, G., et al. The biological activity of undenatured dietary whey proteins: role of glutathione. Clin Invest Med. 14(4):296-309, 1991.
15. Park, Y. J., et al. Quantitation of carnosine in humans plasma after dietary consumption of beef. J Agric Food Chem. 53(12):4736-4739, 2005.
16. Nakamura, Y., et al. Cancer Letters. 157(2):193-200, 2000.
17. Chamila Nimalaratne, Daise Lopes-Lutz, Andreas Schieber, Jianping Wu. **Free aromatic amino acids in egg yolk show antioxidant properties.** *Food Chemistry*, 2011; 129 (1): 155 DOI: 10.1016/j.foodchem.2011.04.058

1.  **Brain Destroying Poisons**

2.  Mullenix, P. J., et al. Neurotoxicity of sodium fluoride in rats. Neurotoxicol Teratol. 17(2):169-177, 1995.
3.  Knivsberg, A. M., et al. A randomised, controlled study of dietary intervention in autistic syndromes. Nutr Neurosci. 5(4):251-261, 2002.
4.  Reichelt, K. L., et al. Gluten, milk proteins and autism: dietary intervention effects on behavior and peptide secretion. J Appl Nutr. 42(1):1-11, 1990.
5.  Hadjivassiliou, M., et al. Headache and CNS white matter abnormalities associated with gluten sensitivity. Neurology. 56(3):385-388, 2001.
6.  Divi, R. L., et al. Anti-thyroid isoflavones from soybean: isolation, characterization, and mechanisms of action. Biochem Pharmacol. 54(10):1087-1096, 1997.
7.  La Rue, A., et al. Nutritional status and cognitive functioning in a normally aging sample: a 6-y reassessment. American Journal of Clinical Nutrition. 65(1):20-29, 1997.
8.  N. Cherbuin, P. Sachdev, K. J. Anstey. **Higher normal fasting plasma glucose is associated with hippocampal atrophy: The PATH Study.** *Neurology*, 2012; 79 (10): 1019 DOI: 10.1212/WNL.0b013e31826846de
9.  Crapper, D. R., et al. Aluminium, neurofibrillary degeneration and Alzheimer's disease. Brain. 99(1):67-80, 1976.
10. Doll, R. Review: Alzheimer's disease and environmental aluminium. Age Ageing. 22(2):138-153, 1993.
11. Graves, A. B., et al. The association between aluminum-containing products and Alzheimer's disease. J Clin Epidemiol. 43(1):35-44, 1990.
12. Jansson, E. T. Aluminum exposure and Alzheimer's disease. Journal of Alzheimer's Disease. 3(6):541-549, 2001.
13. R. Agrawal, F. Gomez-Pinilla. **'Metabolic syndrome' in the brain: deficiency in omega-3 fatty acid exacerbates dysfunctions in insulin receptor signalling and cognition.** *The Journal of Physiology*, 2012; 590 (10): 2485 DOI: 10.1113/jphysiol.2012.230078
14. Calderon, J., et al. Influence of fluoride exposure on reaction time and visuospatial organization in children. Annual Conference of the International Society of Environmental Epidemiology. Epidemiology. 11(4):S153, 2000.
15. Mullenix, P. J., et al. Neurotoxicity of sodium fluoride in rats. Neurotoxicol Teratol. 17(2):169-177, 1995.
16. Bhatnagar, M., et al. Neurotoxicity of fluoride: neurodegeneration in hippocampus of female mice. Indian J Exp Biol. 40(5):546-554, 2002.
17. Mullenix, P. J., et al. Neurotoxicity of sodium fluoride in rats. Neurotoxicol Teratol. 17(2):169-177, 1995.
18. Lu, Y., et al. Effect of high-fluoride water on intelligence of children. Fluoride. 33(2):74-78, 2000.
19. Tang, Q. Q., et al. Fluoride and children's intelligence: a meta-analysis. Biol Trace Elem Res. 2008.
20. Luke, J., et al. Fluoride deposition in the aged human pineal gland. Caries Res. 35(2):125-128, 2001.

21. Morris, M. C., et al. Dietary fats and the risk of incident Alzheimer disease. Archives of Neurology. 60(2):194-200, 2003.
22. Dopeshwarkar, G. A. Nutrition and Brain Development. New York, USA: Plenum Press, 1981:70-73.
23. Chow, C., et al. Fatty Acids in Foods and their Health Implications. Marcek Dekker Inc. New York, USA. 1992:889.
24. Hibbeln, J., et al. Dietary polyunsaturated fatty acids and depression: when cholesterol does not satisfy. American Journal of Clinical Nutrition. 62:1-9, 1995.
25. Kiecolt-Glaser, J. K., et al. Depressive symptoms, omega-6:omega-3 fatty acids, and inflammation in older adults. Psychosom Med. 2007.
26. Zhen Cong, Du Feng, Yin Liu, M. Christina Esperat.**Sedentary Behaviors Among Hispanic Children: Influences of Parental Support in a School Intervention Program**. *American Journal of Health Promotion*, 2012; 26 (5): 270 DOI: 10.4278/ajhp.100226-QUAN-60
27. Luís Lopes, Rute Santos, Beatriz Pereira, Vítor Pires Lopes. **Associations between sedentary behavior and motor coordination in children**. *American Journal of Human Biology*, 2012; DOI: 10.1002/ajhb.22310
28. J. Henson, T. Yates, S. J. H. Biddle, C. L. Edwardson, K. Khunti, E. G. Wilmot, L. J. Gray, T. Gorely, M. A. Nimmo, M. J. Davies. **Associations of objectively measured sedentary behaviour and physical activity with markers of cardiometabolic health**. *Diabetologia*, 2013 DOI: 10.1007/s00125-013-2845-9
29. Bernard M. F. M. Duvivier, Nicolaas C. Schaper, Michelle A. Bremers, Glenn van Crombrugge, Paul P. C. A. Menheere, Marleen Kars, Hans H. C. M. Savelberg. **Minimal Intensity Physical Activity (Standing and Walking) of Longer Duration Improves Insulin Action and Plasma Lipids More than Shorter Periods of Moderate to Vigorous Exercise (Cycling) in Sedentary Subjects When Energy Expenditure Is Comparable**. *PLoS ONE*, 2013; 8 (2): e55542 DOI: 10.1371/journal.pone.0055542
30. P. T. Katzmarzyk, I.-M. Lee. **Sedentary behaviour and life expectancy in the USA: a cause-deleted life table analysis**. *BMJ Open*, 2012; 2 (4): e000828 DOI:10.1136/bmjopen-2012-000828
31. Di Paolo, N., et al. High doses of water increase the purifying capacity of the kidneys. Int J Artif Organs. 30(12):1109-1115, 2007.
32. Jequier, E., et al. Water as an essential nutrient: the physiological basis of hydration. Eur J Clin Nutr. 2009.
33. Clark, N. Water: the ultimate nutrient. Phys Sports Med. 23:32g-32h, 1997.
34. G. J. Haeffel, J. L. Hames. **Cognitive Vulnerability to Depression Can Be Contagious**. *Clinical Psychological Science*, 2013; DOI: 10.1177/2167702613485075
35. Cedrola, S., et al. Inorganic mercury changes the fate of murine CNS stem cells. FASEB J. March 28, 2003.

36. Olivieri, G., et al. Mercury induces cell cytotoxicity and oxidative stress and increases beta-amyloid secretion and tau phosphorylation in SHSY5Y neuroblastoma cells. J Neurochem. 74(1):231-236, 2000.
37. Geier, D. A., et al. Mitochondrial dysfunction, impaired oxidative-reduction activity, degeneration, and death in human neuronal and fetal cells induced by low-level exposure to thimerosal and other metal compounds. Toxicological & Environmental Chemistry. 91(4):735-749, 2009.
38. Kuroda, Y. Aggregation of amyloid beta-protein and its neurotoxicity: enhancement by aluminum and other metals. Tohoku J Exp Med. 3(174):263-268, 1994.
39. Jansson, E. T. Aluminum exposure and Alzheimer's disease. Journal of Alzheimer's Disease. 3(6):541-549, 2001.
40. Kuroda, Y. Aggregation of amyloid beta-protein and its neurotoxicity: enhancement by aluminum and other metals. Tohoku J Exp Med. 3(174):263-268, 1994.
41. Karen Matthews et al. **Sleep Duration and Insulin Resistance in Healthy Black and White Adolescents.***Sleep*, October 2012
42. Ines Wilhelm, Michael Rose, Kathrin I Imhof, Björn Rasch, Christian Büechel, Jan Born. **The sleeping child outplays the adult's capacity to convert implicit into explicit knowledge**. *Nature Neuroscience*, 2013; DOI:10.1038/nn.3343
43. Hogenkamp PS et al. **Acute sleep deprivation increases portion size and affects food choice in young men.***Psychoneuroendocrinology*, in press
44. G. J. Haeffel, J. L. Hames. **Cognitive Vulnerability to Depression Can Be Contagious**. *Clinical Psychological Science*, 2013; DOI: 10.1177/2167702613485075

**Brain Boosting Superfoods**

1. White, A. M., et al. Vinegar ingestion at bedtime moderates waking glucose concentrations in adults with well-controlled type 2 diabetes. Diabetes Care. 30(11):2814-2815, 2007.
2. Cummings, J. H., et al. The control and consequences of bacterial fementation in the human colon: a review. Journal of Applied Bacteriology. 70:443-459, 1991.
3. Topping, D. L. Short-chain fatty acids produced by intestinal bacteria. Asia Pacific Journal of Clinical Nutrition. 5:15-19, 1996.
4. Ostman, E., et al. Vinegar supplementation lowers glucose and insulin responses and increases satiety after a bread meal in healthy subjects. Eur J Clin Nutr. 2005.
5. Fushimi, T., et al. Dietary acetic acid reduces serum cholesterol and triacylglycerols in rats feda cholesterol-rich diet. British Journal of Nutrition. 95(5):916-924, 2006.
6. Kondo, T., et al. Vinegar intake reduces body weight, body fat mass, and serum triglyceride levels in obese Japanese subjects. Biosci Biotechnol Biochem. 2009.

7. Ogawa, N., et al. Acetic acid suppresses the increase in disaccharidase activity that occurs during culture of caco-2 cells. Journal of Nutrition. 130(3):507-513, 2000.
8. Lutz, S. E. Effects of short chain fatty acids and K on absorption of Mg and other cations by the colon and caecum. Z Ernahrungswiss. 29(3):162-168. 1990
9. Auddy, B., et al. A standardized Withania Somnifera extract significantly reduces stress-related parameters in chronically stressed humans: a double-blind, randomized, placebo-controlled study. Journal of the American Nutraceutical Association. 11(1):50-56, 2008.
10. Kuboyama, T., et al. Neuritic regeneration and synaptic reconstruction induced by withanolide A. British Journal of Pharmacology. 144(7):961-971, 2005.
11. Auddy, B., et al. A standardized Withania Somnifera extract significantly reduces stress-related parameters in chronically stressed humans: a double-blind, randomized, placebo-controlled study. Journal of the American Nutraceutical Association. 11(1):50-56, 2008.
12. Bae, J. Y., et al. Bog blueberry anthocyanins alleviate photoaging in ultraviolet-B irradiation-induced human dermal fibroblasts. Mol Nutr Food Res. 2009.
13. Wu, X., et al. Dietary blueberries attenuate atherosclerosis in apolipoprotein e-deficient mice by upregulating antioxidant enzyme expression. Journal of Nutrition. 2010
14. Ronziere, M. C., et al. Influence of some flavonoids on reticulation of collagen fibrils in vitro. Biochem Pharmacol. 30(13):1771-1776, 1981.
15. Passamonti, S., et al. Fast access of some grape pigments to the brain. J Agric Food Chem. 53(18):7029-7034, 2005.
16. Joseph, J. A., et al. Reversals of age-related declines in neuronal signal transduction, cognitive, and motor behavioral deficits with blueberry, spinach, or strawberry dietary supplementation. Journal of Neuroscience. 19(18):8114-8121, 1999.
17. Stromberg, I., et al. Blueberry- and spirulina-enriched diets enhance striatal dopamine recovery and induce a rapid, transient microglia activation after injury of the rat nigrostriatal dopamine system. Exp Neurol. 196(2):298-307, 2005.
18. Ramirez, M. R., et al. Effect of lyophilised Vaccinium berries on memory, anxiety and locomotion in adult rats. Pharmacol Res. 2005.
19. Goyarzu, P., et al. Blueberry supplemented diet: effects on object recognition memory and nuclear factor-kappa B levels in aged rats. Nutritional Neuroscience 7(2):75-83, 2004.
20. Krikorian, R., et al. Blueberry supplementation improves memory in older adults. J Agric Food Chem. 2010.
21. Andres-Lacueva, C., et al. Anthocyanins in aged blueberry-fed rats are found centrally and may enhance memory. Nutr Neurosci. 8(2):111-120, 2005.
22. Joseph, J. A., et al. Dopamine and abeta-induced stress signaling and decrements in ca;{2+} buffering in primary neonatal hippocampal cells are antagonized by blueberry extract. J Alzheimers Dis. 11(4):433-446, 2007.

23. Flammer, A. J., et al. Dark chocolate improves coronary vasomotion and reduces platelet reactivity. Circulation. 116(21):2376-2382, 2007.
24. Francis, S. T., et al. The effect of flavanol-rich cocoa on the fMRI response to a cognitive task in healthy young people. J Cardiovasc Pharmacol. 47(Supplement 2):S215-S220, 2006.
25. Scholey, A. B., et al. Consumption of cocoa flavanols results in acute improvements in mood and cognitive performance during sustained mental effort. J Psychopharmacol. 2009.
26. Cady, R. J., et al. Cocoa-enriched diets enhance expression of phosphatases and decrease expression of inflammatory molecules in trigeminal ganglion neurons. Brain Research. 2010.
27. Hlebowicz, J., et al. Effect of cinnamon on postprandial blood glucose, gastric emptying, and satiety in healthy subjects. American Journal of Clinical Nutrition. 85(6):1552-1556, 2007.
28. Peng, X., et al. Beneficial effects of cinnamon proanthocyanidins on the formation of specific advanced glycation endproducts and methylglyoxal-induced impairment on glucose consumption. J Agric Food Chem. 58(11):6692-6696, 2010.
29. Couturier, K., et al. Cinnamon improves insulin sensitivity and alters the body composition in an animal model of the metabolic syndrome. Arch Biochem Biophys. 2010.
30. Qin, B., et al. Cinnamon: potential role in the prevention of insulin resistance, metabolic syndrome, and type 2 diabetes. J Diabetes Sci Technol. 4(3):685-693, 2010.
31. Solomon, T. P., et al. Changes in glucose tolerance and insulin sensitivity following 2 weeks of daily cinnamon ingestion in healthy humans. European Journal of Applied Physiology. 2009.
32. Peterson, D. W., et al. Cinnamon extract inhibits Tau aggregation associated with Alzheimer's disease in vitro. J Alzheimers Dis. 17(3):585-597, 2009.
33. Vinson, J. A., et al. Comparative bioavailability to humans of ascorbic acid alone or in a citrus extract. American Journal of Clinical Nutrition. 48(3):601-604, 1988.
34. Miller, M. J. Injuries to athletes. Evaluation of ascorbic acid and water soluble citrus bioflavonoids in the prophylaxis of injuries in athletes. Med Times. 88:313-314, 1960.
35. Minato, K., et al. Lemon flavonoid, eriocitrin, suppresses exercise-induced oxidative damage in rat liver. Life Sciences. 72(14):1609-1616, 2003.
36. Garg, A., et al. Chemistry and pharmacology of the citrus bioflavonoid hesperidin. Phytotherapy Research. 15(8):655-669, 2001.
37. Geroulakos, G., et al. Controlled studies of Daflon 500 mg in chronic venous insufficiency. Angiology. 45(6 Part 2):549-553, 1994.
38. Friesenecker, B., et al. Oral administration of purified micronized flavonoid fraction suppresses leukocyte adhesion in ischemia-reperfusion injury: in vivo observations in the hamster skin fold. Int J Microcirc Clin Exp. 14(1-2):50-55, 1994.

39. Hwang, S. L., et al. Neuroprotective effects of the citrus flavanones against H2O2-induced cytotoxicity in PC12 cells. J Agric Food Chem. 56(3):859-864, 2008.
40. Nagase, H., et al. Mechanism of neurotrophic action of nobiletin in PC12D cells. Biochemistry. 44(42):13683-13691, 2005.
41. Nagase, H., et al. Nobiletin and its related flavonoids with CRE-dependent transcription-stimulating and neuritegenic activities. Biochem Biophys Res Commun. 337(4):1330-1336, 2005.
42. Nakajima, A., et al. Nobiletin, a citrus flavonoid that improves memory impairment, rescues bulbectomy-induced cholinergic neurodegeneration in mice. J Pharmacol Sci. 105(1):122-126, 2007.
43. Lagrue, E., et al. Edematous syndromes caused by capillary hyperpermeability. J Mal Vasc. 14(3):231-235, 1989.
44. ernandez, S. P., et al. The flavonoid glycosides, myricitrin, gossypin and naringin exert anxiolytic action in mice. Neurochem Res. 2009.
45. Caudill, M. A., et al. Pre- and postnatal health: evidence of increased choline needs. J Am Diet Assoc. 110(8):1198-1206, 2010.
46. Buchman, A. L., et al. Verbal and visual memory improve after choline supplementation in long-term total parenteral nutrition: a pilot study. J Parenter Enteral Nutr. 25(1):30-35, 2001.
47. Babb, S. M., et al. Oral choline increases choline metabolites in human brain. Psychiatry Res. 130(1):1-9, 2004.
48. Liu, N., et al. [Effect of Zingiber Officinale Rosc on lipid peroxidation in hyperlipidemia rats.] Wei Sheng Yan Jiu. 32(1):22-23, 2003.
49. Eckmann, F., et al. [Cerebral insufficiency--treatment with Ginkgo-biloba extract. Time of onset of effect in a double-blind study with 60 inpatients]. Fortschr Med. 108(29):57-560, 1990.
50. Dumont, E., et al. Protection of polyunsaturated fatty acids against iron-dependent lipid peroxidation by a Ginkgo biloba extract (EGb 761). Methods Find Exp Clin Neurosciences. 17:83-88, 1995.
51. Park, Y. J., et al. Quantitation of carnosine in humans plasma after dietary consumption of beef. J Agric Food Chem. 53(12):4736-4739, 2005.
52. Rule, D. C., K. S. Brought on, S. M. Shellito, and G. Maiorano. "Comparison of Muscle Fatty Acid Profiles and Cholesterol Concentrations of Bison, Beef Cattle, Elk, and Chicken." J Anim Sci 80, no. 5 (2002): 1202-11.
53. Duckett, S. K., D. G. Wagner, et al. (1993). "Effects of time on feed on beef nutrient composition." J Anim Sci 71(8): 2079-88.
54. Lopez-Bote, C. J., R.Sanz Arias, A.I. Rey, A. Castano, B. Isabel, J. Thos (1998). "Effect of free-range feeding on omega-3 fatty acids and alpha-tocopherol content and oxidative stability of eggs." Animal Feed Science and Technology 72: 33-40.
55. Dhiman, T. R., G. R. Anand, et al. (1999). "Conjugated linoleic acid content of milk from cows fed different diets." J Dairy Sci82(10): 2146-56. Interestingly, when the pasture was machine-harvested and then fed to the animals as hay, the cows produced far less CLA than when they were grazing on that pasture, even though the hay was made from the very same grass. The fat that the animals use to produce CLA is oxidized during the

wilting, drying process. For maximum CLA, animals need to be grazing living pasture.
56. Ip, C, J.A. Scimeca, et al. (1994) "Conjugated linoleic acid. A powerful anti-carcinogen from animal fat sources." p. 1053. Cancer74(3 suppl):1050-4.
57. Scalbert, A., et al. Dietary intake and bioavailability of polyphenols. Journal of Nutrition. 130(8 Supplement):2073S-2085S, 2000.
58. Slimestead, R., et al. Onions: a source of unique dietary flavonoids. J Agric Food Chem. 2007.
59. Hollman, P. C., et al. Relative bioavailability of the antioxidant flavonoid quercetin from various foods in man. FEBS Lett. 418(1-2):152-156, 1997.
60. Afanas'ev, I. B., et al. Chelating and free radical scavenging mechanisms of inhibitory action of rutin and quercetin in lipid peroxidation. Biochemical Pharmacology. 38(11):1763-1769, 1989.
61. Evans, G. W., et al. Chromium picolinate increases membrane fluidity and rate of insulin internalization. J Inorg Biochem. 46(4):243-250, 1992.
62. A scientific review: the role of chromium in insulin resistance. Diabetes Educ. Supplement:2-14, 2004.
63. Preuss, H. G., et al. Protective effects of a novel niacin-bound chromium complex and a grape seed proanthocyanidin extract on advancing age and various aspects of syndrome X. Annals of the New York Academy of Sciences, USA. 957:250-259, 2002.
64. Jimbo, D., et al. Effect of aromatherapy on patients with Alzheimer's disease. Psychogeriatrics. 9(4):173-179, 2009.
65. Cartford, M. C., et al. Eighteen-month-old Fischer 344 rats fed a spinach-enriched diet show improved delay classical eyeblink conditioning and reduced expression of tumor necrosis factor alpha (TNFalpha) and TNFbeta in the cerebellum. J Neurosci. 22(14):5813-5816, 2002.
66. Careri, M., et al. Supercritical fluid extraction for liquid chromatographic determination of carotenoids in Spirulina Pacifica algae: a chemometric approach. J Chromatogr. 912:61-71, 2001.
67. Aruna, K., et al. Plant products as protective agents against cancer. Indian J Exp Biol. 28(11):1008-1011, 1990.
68. White, E. L., et al. Screening of potential cancer preventing chemicals for induction of glutathione in rat liver cells. Oncol Rep. 5(2):507-512, 1998.
69. Wang, R., et al. Curcumin protects against glutamate excitotoxicity in rat cerebral cortical neurons by increasing brain-derived neurotrophic factor level and activating TrkB. Brain Res. 2008.
70. Jiang, J., et al. Neuroprotective effect of curcumin on focal cerebral ischemic rats by preventing blood-brain barrier damage. Eur J Pharmacol. 2007.
71. Stillwell, W., et al. Docosahexaenoic acid: membrane properties of a unique fatty acid. Chem Phys Lipids. 126(1):1-27, 2003.
72. Naguib, Y. M. Antioxidant activities of astaxanthin and related carotenoids. J Agric Food Chem. 48(4):1150-1154, 2000.
73. Ono, A., et al. [A 13-week subchronic oral toxicity study of haematococcus color in F344 rats.] Kokuritsu Iyakuhin Shokuhin Eisei Kenkyusho Hokoku. 117:91-98, 1999.

74. Tsuneto, I., et al. ,Effects of astaxanthin on eyestrain induced by accommodative dysfunction. Journal of the Eye. 23(6):829-834, 2006.
75. Chang, C. H., et al. Astaxanthine secured apoptotic death of PC12 cells induced by beta-amyloid peptide 25-35: its molecular action targets. J Med Food. 13(3):548-556, 2010.
76. Hussein, G., et al. Antihypertensive and neuroprotective effects of astaxanthin in experimental animals. Biol Pharm Bull. 28(1):47-52, 2005.
77. Ikeda, Y., et al. Protective effects of astaxanthin on 6-hydroxydopamine-induced apoptosis in human neuroblastoma SH-SY5Y cells. Journal of Neurochemistry. 107(6):1730-1740, 2008.
78. Cao, Y., et al. Glutamine enhances gut glutathione production. J Parenter Enteral Nutr. 22(4):224-227, 1998.
79. Flaring, U. B., et al. Glutamine attenuates post-traumatic glutathione depletion in human muscle. Clin Sci. 104(3):275-282, 2003.
80. Bounous, G., et al. The biological activity of undenatured dietary whey proteins: role of glutathione. Clin Invest Med. 14(4):296-309, 1991.
81. Bounous, G. Whey protein concentrate (WPC) and glutathione modulation in cancer treatment. Anticancer Research. 20(6C):4785-4792, 2000.
82. Bounous, G., et al. The influence of dietary whey protein on tissue glutathione and the diseases of aging. Clin Invest Med. 12(6):343-349, 1989.

**Chronic Stress Damages Brain Function**

1. Anderson, Barbara L, Kiecolt-Glaser, Janice K, and Glaser, Ronald. A Biobehavior Model of Cancer Stress and Disease Course. Am Psychol. 1994 May; 49(5): 389-404.
1. McEwen BS. Plasticity of the hippocampus: adaptation to chronic stress and allostaticload. Ann N Y Acad Sci. 2001 Mar;933:265-77.
2. Taekwan Lee, Tim Jarome, Shi-Jiang Li, Jeansok J. Kim, and Fred J. Helmstetter. Chronic stress selectively reduces hippocampal volume in rats: a longitudinal MRI study. Neurorerport. 2009 November 25; 20(17): 1554-1558.
3. Weiss, C.S. Depression and immunoincompetence: A review of the literature.Psychological Bulletin 1992; 111:475-489. [PubMed: 1594722].
4. Fidelibus, J. An overview of neuroimmunomodulation and a possible correlation with musculoskeletal system function. JMPT 1989; 12 (4): 289-292.
5. Haavik Taylor, H., Holt, K., Murphy, B.A., Exploring the neurmodulatory effects of the vertebral subluxation and chiropractic care. The Chiropractors Association of Austrailia (CAA) Policy Forum and Scientific Symposium, November 2009.
6. Haavik Taylor H, Holt KR, Murphy B. (2010) Chiropractors' Association of Austrailia Scientific Symposium 2009 first prize award winning paper: Exploring the neuromodulatory effects of the vertebral subluxation and chiropractic care. Chiropractic Journal of Austrailia, 40(1):37-44.

7. Haavik Taylor, H. & Murphy B.A. (2007) Cervical spine manipulation alters sensorimotor integration: A somatosensory evoked potential study Clinical Neurophysiology, 118(2): 391-402.
8. Haavik Tayor H and Murphy B. (2007) Transient modulation of intracortical inhibition following spinal manipulation. Chiropractic Journal of Austrailia, 37:106-116
9. Haavik Taylor, H., Murphy, B.A. Spinal Manipulation alters central integration of dual somatosensory input observed following motor training. ACC Research Agenda Conference, Las Vegas, USA, March 12-14, 2009, JCA 23(1):83.
10. Haavik Taylor H and Murphy B. (2008) Altered sensorimotor integration with cervical spine manipulation. Journal of Manipulative and Physiological Therapeutics, 31(2): 115-126.
11. Haavik, Taylor H and Murphy, B. (2010) Altered Central Integration of Dual Somatosensory input Following Cervical Spine Manipulation. Journal of Manipulative and Physiological Therapeutics, 33(3):178-188
12. Haavik Taylor H, Murphy B.A., (2010) The effects of spinal manipulation on central integration of dual somatosensory input observed following motor training: A crossover study. Journal of Manipulative and Physiological Therapeutics 33(4):271-262.
13. Haavik Taylor H. Murphy, B.A. (in press) Subclinical neck pain and the effects of cervical adjustments on elbow joint position sense. Journal of Manipulative and Physiological Therapeutics.
14. Masarsky CS, Todres-Masarsky M. Effect of a single chiropractic adjustment on divergent thinking and creative output: a pilot study, Part 1. Chiropr J Aust 2010;40:57-62.
15. Slosberg, M. Effects of altered afferent articular input on sensation, proprioception, muscle tone, and sympathetic reflex responses. JMPT 1988; 11(5): 400-408.
16. Yates et al. Descending pathways necessary for vestibular influences on sympathetic and respiratory outflow. Am. J. Physiol. 1995; 689: 197-206.

**Brain Based Movement and Exercise**

1. Boyd Eaton M.D., Melvin Konner Ph.D., M.D. and Marjorie Shostak. Stone agers in the fast lane: Chronic degenerative diseases in evolutionary perspective. 1988; Am. J. Med. 84, 739-749
2. Cordain L, Gotshall RW, Eaton SB, Eaton SB 3rd. Physical Activity, energy expenditure and fitness: an evolutionary perspective. Int J Sports Med. 1998 Jul;19(5):328-35.
3. Eaton, Cordain and Lindeberg. Evolutionary Health Promotion: A Consideration of Common Counterarguments. Preventative Medicine 2002 (34) 119-123.
4. F.W. Booth, Manu V Chakravarthy, and Espen E Spangenburg. Exercise and gene expression: physiological regulation of the human genome through physical activity. J Appl Physiol 543, 399-411

5. Frank W. Booth, Manu V. Chakravarthy, Scott E. Gordon, and Espen E. Spargenburg. Waging war on physical inactivity: using modern molecular ammunition against an ancient enemy J Appl Physiol 93: 3-30, 2002.
6. Roberts, C.K. & Barnard, J.B. Effects of exercise and diet on chronic disease. 2005 J. Appl Physiol 98 3-30

**SuperCharged Brain Strategies**

1. Akiyama K, Sutoo D. Effect of different frequencies of music on blood pressure regulation in spontaneously hypertensive rats. Neurosci Lett. 2011 Jan 3;487(1):58-60. doi: 10.1016/j.neulet.2010.09.073. Epub 2010 Oct 12.
2. Anson, R. M., Guo, Z, de Cabo, R., Iyun, T., Rios, M., Hagepanos, A., Ingram, D. K., Lane, M. A. & Mattson, M. P. (2003, April 30). Intermittent fasting dissociates beneficial effects of dietary restriction on glucose metabolism and neuronal resistance to injury from calorie intake. National Academy of Sciences Online Early Edition.
3. Al-Hader, A.A., Hasan, Z.A., Aqel, M.B. (1994). Hyperglycemic and insulin release inhibitory effects of rosmarinus officinalis. Journal of Ethnopharmacology, 43, 217,22.
4. Arlinger, S.; Elberling, C.; Bak, C.; Kofoed, B.; Lebech, J.; Saermark, K. (1982). "Cortical magnetic fields evoked by frequency glides of a continuous tone". EEG & Clinical Neurophysiology 54 (6): 642–653. doi:10.1016/0013-4694(82)90118-3.
5. Bahadori B, McCarty MF, Barroso-Aranda J, Gustin JC, Contreras F. A "mini-fast with exercise" protocol for fat loss. Med Hypotheses. 2009 Oct;73(4):619-22. doi: 10.1016/j.mehy.2008.09.063. Epub 2009 Jul 3.
6. Balion C, Griffith LE, Strifler L, Henderson M, Patterson C, Heckman G, Llewellyn DJ, Raina P. Vitamin D, cognition, and dementia: a systematic review and meta-analysis. Neurology. 2012 Sep 25;79(13):1397-405.
7. Barbagallo M, Belvedere M, Di Bella G, Dominguez LJ. Altered ionized magnesium levels in mild-to-moderate Alzheimer's disease. Magnes Res. 2011 Sep;24(3):S115-21. doi: 10.1684/mrh.2011.0287.
8. Bassett, I. B., Pannowitz, D. L., & Barnetson, R. S. (1990). A comparative study of tea-tree oil versus benzoylperoxide in the treatment of acne. Med J Aust, 153(8), 455-458.
9. Bernardes W, Lucarini R, Tozatti M, Flauzino L, Souza M, Turatti I, Andrade e Silva M, martins C, da Silva Filho A & Cunha W. (2010). Antibacterial activity of the essential oil from Rosmarinus officinalis and its major components against oral pathogens.
10. Bilici M, Yildirim F, Kandil S, et al. "Double-blind, placebo-controlled study of zinc sulfate in the treatment of attention deficit hyperactivity disorder." Prog Neuropsychopharmacol Biol Psychiatry. 2004 Jan;28(1):181-90
11. Breig A. Adverse Mechanical Tension in the Central Nervous System: An Analysis of Cause and Effect: Relief by Functional Neurosurgery. New York, NY: J. Wiley; 1978.

12. Brotons M, Marti P. Music therapy with Alzheimer's patients and their family caregivers: a pilot project. J Music Ther. 2003 Summer;40(2):138-50.
13. Brown, S.; Martinez, M.J.; Parsons, L.M. (2006). "Music and language side by side in the brain: a PET study of the generation of melodies and sentences". European Journal of Neuroscience 23 (10): 2791–2803. doi:10.1111/j.1460-9568.2006.04785.x.
14. Bronwen Martin,a,* Mark P. Mattson,a,b and Stuart Maudsley. Caloric restriction and intermittent fasting: Two potential diets for successful brain aging. Ageing Res Rev. 2006 August; 5(3): 332–353. Published online 2006 August 8. doi: 10.1016/j.arr.2006.04.002
15. Buckle, J. (2007). Literature review: should nursing take aromatherapy more seriously? British Journal of Nursing, 16, (2), 116-120.
16. Cappello, G, Spezzaferro, M, Grossi, L, et al. (2007). Peppermint oil (Mintoil) in the treatment of irritable bowel syndrome: A prospective double blind placebo-controlled randomized trial. Digestive & Liver Disease, 39(6), 530-536.
17. C.F. Garland et al. Vitamin D supplement doses and serum 25-hydroxyvitmain D in the range association with cancer prevention. Anticancer Research, Vo. 31, 2011, p. 607.
18. Christie, Ronald V. Some types of respiration in the neuroses. QJM 4.4 (1935): 427-428.
19. Chung, M, Cho, S, Bhuiyan, M, Kim, K & Lee, S. (2010). Anti-diabetic effects of lemon balm (Melissa officinalis) essential oil on glucose- and lipid-regulating enzymes in type 2 diabetic mice.British J of Nutrition, 104 (2), 180-188.
20. CLAUDIO PACCHETTI, MD, FRANCESCA MANCINI, MD, ROBERTO AGLIERI, CIRA FUNDARO`, MD, EMILIA MARTIGNONI, MD, AND GIUSEPPE NAPPI, MD. Active Music Therapy in Parkinson's Disease: An Integrative Method for Motor and Emotional Rehabilitation. Psychosomatic Medicine 62:386–393 (2000).
21. Cohen, Mandel E., and Paul D. White. Studies of breathing, pulmonary ventilation and subjective awareness of shortness of breath (dyspnea) in neurocirculatory asthenia, effort syndrome, anxiety neurosis. Journal of Clinical Investigation 26.3 (1947): 520.
22. Cotman, Carl W, Berchtold, Nichole C, Christie, Lori-Ann. Exercise builds brain health: key roles of growth factor cascades and inflammation.
23. Den'etsu Sutoo*, Kayo Akiyama. Music improves dopaminergic neurotransmission: demonstration based on the effect of music on blood pressure regulation. Institute of Medical Science, University of Tsukuba, Tsukuba, Ibaraki 305-8575, Japan.
24. Duan, W., Guo, Z., Jaing, H., Ware, M., Li, X-J., & Mattson, M. P. (2003). Dietary Restriction Normalizes Glucose Metabolism and Brain-Derived Neurotrophic Factor Levels, Slows Disease Progression and Increases Survival in Huntington Mutant Mice. Proceedings of the National Academy of Sciences Online Early Edition.

25. Dwivedi, C. & Zhang, Y. (1999). Sandalwood oil prevents skin tumour development in CD1 mice. European Journal of Cancer Prevention, 8, 449-55.
26. Flanagan MF. Relationship between CSF and fluid dynamics in the neural canal. J Manipulative Physiol Ther. 1988;11(6):489-492.
27. Gae'tan Chevalier, PhD,1 Stephen T. Sinatra, MD, FACC, FACN,2 James L. Oschman, PhD,3 and Richard M. Delany, MD, FACC. Earthing (Grounding) the Human Body Reduces Blood Viscosity—a Major Factor in Cardiovascular Disease. THE JOURNAL OF ALTERNATIVE AND COMPLEMENTARY MEDICINE Volume 19, Number 2, 2013, pp. 102–110a. DOI: 10.1089/acm.2011.0820.
28. Glassey DJ. The anatomy and physiology of CSF circulation. Presented at: Sacro Occipital Research Society International; April 8, 2006; St. Louis, MO.
29. Godfrey, RJ, Whyte, GP, Buckley, J, Quinlivan, R. The role of lactate in the exercise-induced human growth hormone response: evidence from McArdle disease. Br J Sports Med. 2009 Jul;43(7):521-5. doi: 10.1136/bjsm.2007.041970. Epub 2008 Jan 9.
30. Hajhashemi, V., Ghannadi, A., & Sharif, B. (2003). Anti-inflammatory and analgesic properties of the leaf extracts and essential oil of lavandula angustifolia mill. Journal of Ethnopharmacology, 89(1), 67-71.
31. Han, J. N., et al. Unsteadiness of breathing in patients with hyperventilation syndrome and anxiety disorders. European Respiratory Journal 10.1 (1997): 167-176.
32. Hansen, T., Hansen, B., Ringdal, G. (2006). Does aromatherapy massage reduce job-related stress? Results from a randomized, controlled trial. International Journal of Aromatherapy, June, 16, (2), 89-94.
33. Haze, S, Sakai, K & Gozu, Y. (2002). Effects of fragrance inhalation on sympathetic activity in normal adults. Japanese Journal of Pharmacology, 90, 247-253.
34. Hillman, Charles H., Erickson, Kirk I., Arthur F. Kramer. Be smart, exercise your heart: exercise effects on brain and cognition. Nature Reviews and Neuroscience 9, 58-65 (January 2008). doi:10.1038/nrn2298.
35. Hiramatsu K, Yamada T, Katakura M. Acute effects of cold on blood pressure, renin-angiotensin-aldosterone system, catecholamines and adrenal steroids in men. Clin Exp Pharmacol Physiol 1984; 11:171–9.
36. Iwaki, Tatsuya; Hayashi, Mitsuo; Hori, Tadao. (1997). Changes in alpha band EEG activity in the frontal area after stimulation with music of different affective content. Perceptual & Motor Skills, 84:515-526.
37. Jentschke, S.; Koelsch, S.; Sallat, S.; Friederici, A.D. (2008). "Children with specific language impairment also show impairment of music-syntactic processing". Journal of Cognitive Neuroscience 20 (11): 1940–1951. doi:10.1162/jocn.2008.20135.
38. Johnson DG, Hayward JS, Jacobs TP, Collis ML, Eckerson JD, Williams RH. Plasma norepinephrin
39. Raloff. Sunshine vitamin diminishes risk of colds, flu. Science News Online, Feb. 23, 2009.

40. Raloff. The Antibiotic Vitamin. Science News, Vol. 170, Nov. 11, 2006, p. 312.
41. J.E. Manson et al. Vitamin D and prevention of cancer — ready for prime time? New England Journal of Medicine, April 14, 2011, p. 1385.
42. Kawaii S, Tomono Y, Katase E, et al. Antiproliferative effects of the readily extractable fractions prepared from various citrus juices on several cancer cell lines. J Agric Food Chem 1999 Jul;47(7):2509-12. 1999.
43. Khaw KT, Bingham S, Welch A, et al. Relation between plasma ascorbic acid and mortality in men and women in EPIC-Norfolk prospective study: a prospective population study. European Prospective Investigation into Cancer and Nutrition. Lancet. 2001 Mar 3;357(9257):657-63. 2001.
44. Koelsch, S.; Gunter, T.; Friederici, A.D.; Schoger, E. (2000). "Brain indices of music processing: "nonmusicians" are musical". Journal of Cognitive Neuroscience 12 (3): 520–541. doi:10.1162/089892900562183.
45. Koelsch, S., Gunter, T., Cramon, D., Zysset, S., Lohmann, G. & Friederici, A. (2002). "Bach Speaks: A Cortical Language-Network Serves the Processing of Music". NeuroImage 17 (2): 956–966. doi:10.1006/nimg.2002.1154.
46. Kroger, Susan M., Chapin,Kathryn, Brotons, Melissa. Is Music Therapy an Effective Intervention for Dementia? Journal of Music Therapy, XXXVI (1), 1999, 2-25. 1999 by th American Music Therapy Association.
47. Kurl S, Tuomainen TP, Laukkanen JA et al. Plasma vitamin C modifies the association between hypertension and risk of stroke. Stroke 2002 Jun;33(6):1568-73. 2002.
48. Lahl, Olaf; Wispel, Christiane; Willigens, Bernadette; Pietrowsky, Reinhard (2008). "An ultra short episode of sleep is sufficient to promote declarative memory performance". Journal of Sleep Research 17 (1): 3–10.
49. Lehrner, J., Marwinski, G., Lehr, S., Johren, P., & Deecke, L. (2005). Ambient odors of orange and lavender reduce anxiety and improve mood in a dental office. Physiology & Behavior, 86(1-2), 92-95.
50. Lepping P, Huber M. "Role of zinc in the pathogenesis of attention-deficit hyperactivity disorder: implications for research and treatment."CNS Drugs. 2010 Sep 1;24(9):721-8
51. Liu, X. and Osawa, T. Astaxanthin protects neuronal cells against oxidative damage and is a potent candidate for brain food. Forum Nutr. 2009;61:129-135.
52. Liu, L.F.; Palmer, A.R., Wallace, M.N. (March 2006). "Phase-Locked Responses to Pure Tones in the Inferior Colliculus". Journal of Neurophysiology 95 (3): 1926–1935. doi:10.1152/jn.00497.2005. PMID 16339005.
53. Maas, James B.; Wherry, Megan L. (1998). Miracle Sleep Cure: The Key to a Long Life of Peak Performance. London: Thorsons. ISBN 978-0-7225-3644-5
54. Mattson MP. Energy intake, meal frequency, and health: a neurobiological perspective. Annu Rev Nutr. 2005;25:237-60.
55. Mednick, S. C. et al. (2008). Comparing the benefits of caffeine, naps, and placebo on verb al, motor and perceptual memory. Behavioral Brain Research. 193: 79-86.

56. Miyake Y, Murakami A, Sugiyama Y, et al. Identification of coumarins from lemon fruit (Citrus limon) as inhibitors of in vitro tumor promotion and superoxide and nitric oxide generation. J Agric Food Chem 1999 Aug;47(8):3151-7. 1999. PMID:13130.
57. Moan, J. Dahlback, A. Porojnicu, AC. At what time should one go out in the sun. Advanced Experiments in Medical Biology 2008; 624: 86-88.
58. M.R. von Essen et al. Vitamin D controls T cell antigen receptor signaling and activation of human T cells. Nature Immunology, online March 2010. Doi: 10.1038/ni.1851
59. Muhle C, Weinert D, Falliner A, et al. Dynamic changes of the spinal canal in patients with cervical spondylosis at fl exion and extension using magnetic resonance imaging. Invest Radiol. 1998;33(8):444-449.
60. Nashat Abumaria, Bin Yin, Ling Zhang, Xiang-Yao Li, Tao Chen, Giannina Descalzi, Liangfang Zhao, Matae Ahn, Lin Luo, Chen Ran, Min Zhuo, Guosong Liu. Effects of Elevation of Brain Magnesium on Fear Conditioning, Fear Extinction, and Synaptic Plasticity in the Infralimbic Prefrontal Cortex and Lateral Amygdala. The Journal of Neuroscience, 19 October 2011, 31(42): 14871-14881; doi: 10.1523/JNEUROSCI.3782-11.2011.
61. Nickerson, R.S. (1999). "Enhancing Creativity", in ed. Sternberg, R.J.: Handbook of Creativity. Cambridge University Press.
62. Ober, Clinton A. Grounding the human body to neutralize bioelectrical stress from static electricity and EMFs. ESF Journal, January 2000. http://www.esdjournal.com/articles/cober/ground.htm
63. Pelsser LMJ, Buitelaar JK, Savelkoul HFJ. ADHD as a (non) allergic hypersensitivity disorder: A hypothesis. Pediatr Allergy Immunol 2008 Ó 2008 The Authors DOI: 10.1111/j.1399-3038.2008.00749.x
64. Patterson, R. D.; Uppenkamp, S.; Johnsrude, I. S.; Griffiths, T. D. (2002). "The processing of temporal pitch and melody information in auditory cortex". Neuron 36 (4): 767–776. doi:10.1016/S0896-6273(02)01060-7.
65. Perrin RN. Lymphatic drainage of the neuraxis in chronic fatigue syndrome: a hypothetical model for the cranial rhythmic impulse. J Am Osteopath Assoc. 2007;107(6):218-224.
66. Perry, Stephane. Promoting Motor Function by Exercising the Brain. Brain Sci. 2013, 3(1), 101-122; doi:10.3390/brainsci3010101.
67. Rubenstein E. Relationship of senescence of cerebrospinal fluid circulatory system to dementias of the aged. Lancet. 1998;351(9098):283-285.
68. Skoe, E.; Kraus, N. (June 2010). "Auditory brainstem response to complex sounds: a tutorial". Ear and Hearing 31 (3): 302–324. doi:10.1097/AUD.0b013e3181cdb27
69. Soni M, Kos K, Lang IA, Jones K, Melzer D, Llewellyn DJ. Vitamin D and cognitive function. Scand J Clin Lab Invest Suppl. 2012 Apr;243:79-82. doi: 10.3109/00365513.2012.681969.
70. Tapan Audhya, Ph.D. ROLE OF B VITAMINS IN BIOLOGICAL METHYLATION. Health Diagnostics and Research Institute.
71. Torres Salazar A, Hoheisel J, Youns M & Wink M. (2011). Anti-inflammatory and anti-cancer activities of essential oils and their biological

constituents. International J of Clinical Pharmacology & Therapeutics, 49 (1), 93-95.
72. Tzu-Wei Lin, Yu-Min Kuo. Exercise Benefits Brain Function: The Monoamine Connection. Brain Sci. 2013, 3(1), 39-53; doi: 10.3390/brainsci3010039.
73. Van Proeyen K, Szlufcik K, Nielens H, Pelgrim K, Deldicque L, Hesselink M, Van Veldhoven PP, Hespel P. Training in the fasted state improves glucose tolerance during fat-rich diet. J Physiol. 2010 Nov 1;588(Pt 21):4289-302. doi: 10.1113/jphysiol.2010.196493.
74. Vlachopoulos C, Aznaouridis K, Alexopoulos N, Economou E, Andreadou I, Stefanadis C. Effect of dark chocolate on arterial function in healthy individuals. Am J Hypertens. 2005 Jun;18(6):785-91.
75. Von Bubnoff, A., & Lloyd, J. (2006). Prevention's anti-aging guide: How to take off 10 years or more. Prevention, 58(9), 166-213.
76. Woelk, H & Schlafke, S. (2009). A multi-center, double-blind, randomizsed study of the lavender oil preparation Silexan in comparison to Lorazepam for generalized anxiety disorder. Phytomedicine, 17, 94-99.
77. Wolfe, David. "Superfoods: The Food and Medicine of the Future"; North Atlantic Books, 2009.
78. Zhenyu Yue, Lauren Friedman, Masaaki Komatsu, and Keiji Tanaka. The Cellular Pathways of Neuronal Autophagy and Their Implication in Neurodegenerative Diseases. Biochim Biophys Acta. 2009 September; 1793(9): 1496–1507.

**Brain Boosting Supplements:**

1. Meguid, N. A., et al. Reduced serum levels of 25-hydroxy and 1,25-dihydroxy vitamin D in Egyptian children with autism. J Altern Complement Med. 16(6):641-645, 2010.
2. Kinney, D. K., et al. Environmental risk factors for autism: do they help cause de novo genetic mutations that contribute to the disorder? Med Hypotheses. 74(1):102-106, 2010.
3. Humble, M. B., et al. Low serum levels of 25-hydroxyvitamin D (25-OHD) among psychiatric out-patients in Sweden: Relations with season, age, ethnic origin and psychiatric diagnosis. J Steroid Biochem Mol Biol. 2010.
4. Fernell, E., et al. Serum levels of 25-hydroxyvitamin D in mothers of Swedish and of Somali origin who have children with and without autism. Acta Paediatr. 2010.
5. Cannell, J. J. Autsim and vitamin D. Med Hypotheses. 70(4):750-759, 2007.
6. Cannell, J. J., et al. Use of vitamin D in clinical practice. Alternative Medicine Review. 13(1):6-20, 2008.
7. Llewellyn, D. J., et al. Vitamin D and risk of cognitive decline in elderly persons. Archives of Internal Medicine. 170(13):1135-1141, 2010.

8. Llewellyn, D. J., et al. Serum 25-hydroxyvitamin d concentration and cognitive impairment. Journal of Geriatric Psychiatry and Neurology. 2009.
9. Oudshoorn, C., et al. Higher serum vitamin d(3) levels are associated with better cognitive test performance in patients with Alzheimer's Disease. Dement Geriatr Cogn Disord. 25(6):539-543, 2008.
10. Przybelski, R. J., et al. Is vitamin D important for preserving cognition? A positive correlation of serum 25-hydroxyvitamin D concentration with cognitive function. Arch Biochem Biophys. 460(2):202-205, 2007.
11. Tuohimaa, P., et al. Vitamin D, nervous system and aging. Psychoneuroendocrinology. 2009.
12. Milaneschi, Y., et al. Serum 25-hydroxyvitamin d and depressive symptoms in older women and men.
13. J Clin Endocrinol Metab. 2010.Scorza, F. A., et al. Benefits of sunlight: vitamin D deficiency might increase the risk of sudden unexpected death in epilepsy. Med Hypotheses. 2009
14. Burton, J. M., et al. A phase I/II dose-escalation trial of vitamin D3 and calcium in multiple sclerosis. Neurology. 2010.
15. Knekt, P., et al. Serum vitamin D and the risk of Parkinson disease. Archives of Neurology. 67(7):808-811, 2010.
16. Howard, D. A., et al. Vitamin D and chronic mental illness. Medical Journal of Australia. 184(1):47, 2006.
17. Vieth, R. .Vitamin D and cancer mini-symposium: the risk of additional vitamin D. Ann Epidemiol. 19(7):441-445, 2009.
18. Vieth, R. Vitamin D supplementation, 25-hydroxyvitamin D concentrations, and safety. Am J Clin Nutr. 69(5):842-856, 2005.
19. Heaney, R. P., et al. The Vitamin D requirement in health and disease. J Steroid Biochem Mol Biol. 97(1-2):13-19, 2005.
20. Hanley, D. A., et al. Vitamin D insufficiency in North America. Journal of Nutrition. 135(2):332-337, 2005.
21. Connor, W. E. Importance of n-3 fatty acids in health and disease. American Journal of Clinical Nutrition. 71(1 Supplement):171S-175S, 2000.
22. Lopez-Garcia, E., et al. Consumption of (n-3) fatty acids is related to plasma biomarkers of inflammation and endothelial activation in women. Journal of Nutrition. 134(7):1806-1811, 2004.
23. Lee, S. J., et al. Astaxanthin inhibits nitric oxide production and inflammatory gene expression by suppressing I(kappa)B kinase-dependent NF-kappaB activation. Mol Cells. 16(1):97-105, 2003.
24. Ohgami, K., et al. Effects of astaxanthin on lipopolysaccharide-induced inflammation in vitro and in vivo. Invest Ophthalmol Vis Sci. 44(6):2694-2701, 2003.
25. Chang, C. H., et al. Astaxanthine secured apoptotic death of PC12 cells induced by beta-amyloid peptide 25-35: its molecular action targets. J Med Food. 13(3):548-556, 2010
26. Hussein, G., et al. Antihypertensive and neuroprotective effects of astaxanthin in experimental animals. Biol Pharm Bull. 28(1):47-52, 2005.

27. Tsuneto, I., et al. ,Effects of astaxanthin on eyestrain induced by accommodative dysfunction. Journal of the Eye. 23(6):829-834, 2006.
28. Naguib, Y. M. Antioxidant activities of astaxanthin and related carotenoids. J Agric Food Chem. 48(4):1150-1154, 2000.
29. Kaila, M., et al. Enhancement of the circulating antibody secreting response in human diarrhea by a human Lactobacillus strain. Pediatr Res. 32(2):141-144, 1992
30. Rolfe, R. D., et al. The role of probiotic cultures in the control of gastrointestinal health. Journal of Nutrition. 130(Supplement):396S-402S, 2000.
31. Smith AD, Smith SM, de Jager CA, Whitbread P, Johnston C, et al. (2010) Homocysteine-Lowering by B Vitamins Slows the Rate of Accelerated Brain Atrophy in Mild Cognitive Impairment: A Randomized Controlled Trial. PLoS ONE 5(9): e12244. doi:10.1371/journal.pone.0012244

Made in the USA
Coppell, TX
24 May 2021